Rise Up, Mighty
Man of Valor

Men as Spiritual Leaders
of the Family

Dr. Wayne Parks

XULON PRESS

Table of Contents

Introduction

*I*t seems that we, as men, have forgotten to think on our own. We rely on everyone and everything to do that for us. We have wives to wake us up in the morning and smart phones to remind us of our wedding anniversary. We also allow people to tell us how our marriage should work. We are told to follow our hearts and do what feels good. Since we generally do not have any constant direction, we follow that advice without second thought. Time passes. Because of a lack of standards, marriages are failing, families are falling apart, children are suffering. Men with moral convictions are becoming scarce. Christian men have forgotten our role. We have allowed the world to mold us instead of staying with God's design. This has led to many problems, including children growing up confused and families being redefined to what the culture feels appropriate.

It is time we, as Christian men, rise up! We need to remember why we were created and how we can take back our role as spiritual leader of the home. God gave us authority over this earth through the blood of Christ. Now is the time to remind Satan that his work is limited here. God's kingdom will rise up! It starts with men becoming men and taking responsibility for themselves, their families and their homes! With consistent effort, we can turn our destructive paths around and with God's guidance, reclaim our families for Christ!

Dedication

I dedicate this book to my wife...

Kristen Parks

You ou have allowed me to grow into the man I am today. You have taught me to stay obedient to the voice of God, even when it doesn't always make sense. For this and many other reasons, I will fight every day for the rest of my life to make sure you feel like you are worth fighting for.

For those of you who know me, you understand how much of a miracle this book is. Without the inspiration from God and the vision He has given me, this would not have been possible. I would like to say a special "Thank you" to my wife, Kristen, for staying up with me night after night and painting while I wrote; and for inspiring me to step out of my comfort zone and stay obedient to the call God has given me. Thank you to my daughters for being patient with me while I typed at the kitchen table. A special thank you to Tony and Marianne Gignac for providing an environment for spiritual growth while mentoring Kristen and me on a weekly basis. God has provided a multitude of counselors for me and my family. For these counselors, I am forever grateful.

Acknowledgments

A special acknowledgment goes out to those who were obedient in the call of God who stepped out and trusted me with their gift:

Tony & Marianne Gignac

Matt & Sarah Reid

Craig & Lisa Laubacher

Lance & Juli Mormon

Dr. Dennis & Beverly Jones

George & Tiffany Nowlin

David & Jerica Villanueva

Justin Day

Victor & Rachel Marquez

Jose &Edith Pena

Matt & Kelly Timmons

Greg & Terra Howard

Ben & Barbara Bagdonas

Barbie Bowtique /

McRee Family	Tom & Kathy Baker
Scott & Suzanne Fye	Joseph & Robyn Lendo
Kevin & Christa Baker	Ryan &Kristen Epps
Drs. Keith and	Jason & Melissa Lira
Natalie Wheeler	Colin & Paula Weatherly
Charles & Diane Tovey	Sharon Maruschak
Jim & Laura Costello	John & Kristy Simank
Edward & Sarah Jackson	Blake & April Drew
Jay & Amy Soileau	Philip & Chelsea Garcia
Tim & Michelle Goss	Shawn & Kimberly Robinson
Chris & Lisa Boss	Mario & Alex Vega
Brenda Perkins	Dr. Larry and Crystal
Allison Timm	Charleston
Larry & Carol Parks	Robin Broadway
Mike & Deborah Myers	Steve & Rhonda Haskins
Valerie Laubacher	Lance & Heather Smith

Foreword

$\mathcal{A}$fter a good amount of fighting and denial, I finally gave in and started writing this book. One of my greatest challenges was in thinking I actually had something different to say/share from all the other books out there for men. Quite honestly, there probably isn't anything in this book that you haven't heard or don't already know. However, God continued to speak to me saying some men out there need to hear things both specifically and personally.

I want to ask you to think about two words: Redeemed and Resentful! Which one are you? If you are not sure, look up the meaning of these two words. If you know, I hope you are redeemed! If not, my journey may help you release the resentfulness you hold.

Let me explain. My wife and I were at some dear friends of ours one evening for a study about being <u>Relentless</u> by author John Bevere. Our fourth week or so in the study we began talking to our host and hostess. The topic came up about a men's retreat several years ago. During this retreat, the group had taken a photo of themselves. This photo then scrolled over the screen saver of the host's computer. The host commented that the picture appeared to be more like a photo of a graduating class from a cheaters' college than a seminar on how to stay faithful to your wife and God. When he spoke those words out loud, it was physically painful to me. I knew several of the men he was talking about, and it made me ill thinking of how I had once highly respected these men and the standards they seemingly followed in their marriage. Now, they were divorced because of adultery.

How can a group of men make a commitment in a Men's seminar one moment and in the next, totally break the promise they'd just made? What if they went to this meeting with resentment in their hearts? What if this seminar had been promoted in such a way that they had no choice but to attend because they had been backed into a corner in front of their wives or by their wives? Maybe the pastor announced in front of the congregation that a group of men from the church were going to the seminar and commented, "If you truly love your wife, you'll be there with us!" Who can say no to a promotion like that? They found themselves in a seminar they really did not want to attend because of the bruises in their ribs from their wives. They might have had no intention of cheating on their wives. But this kind of pressure and similar stress can contribute to the frustrations in our lives creating mounting resentment within our hearts.

Am I crazy or not? What man would really have an affair just to get back at his wife for making him sit in a retreat for a weekend? Surely this could not happen. Men don't consciously try to get back at their wives for making them do something they don't want to, right? Or would they? Could being at the seminar be that bad? After all, the seminar offers a chance for true redemption which beats our chances in the garage working on a project, right?

So, are you reading this book because you've been redeemed and just want some more grace and knowledge? Or are you reading this book because you're full of resentment. Maybe someone handed you this book and said, "Dude, YOU need to read this!" Maybe it was a "gift" from your wife. It's just another book in a stack of books someone gave you to read and "better" yourself. Yet, you never thought you needed to be "better" in the first place.

If this is you, and if you're resentful for whatever reason, I want to help you RIGHT NOW! But you must follow these very specific instructions!

1. Take this book and go to a place where you are totally alone-A place where you know you can't be seen or heard by anyone. Places I have gone to are: In my car, in my bedroom closet with my door shut, outside in the backyard of the house. I don't care where you go. JUST GO!

2. Now, I need you to read this prayer OUT LOUD! No, you don't have to scream it. However, I do want you to speak it out loud, so you can hear it. This way Satan can hear it too because he can't read your mind. Only God can. You want Satan to know that you're retaking control of your life. Now speak this! Ready? Here we go.

Father God,

You are the author of life. God, you created me in your own image because you love me and you want me to prosper and conquer. Lord, all good things come from you. And Lord, all things that are bad come from Satan. Satan, in the name of Jesus, I bind you. You Satan, have no authority over me. Lord, You wouldn't create me, redeem me and then hurt me. That would go against Your Word and Your Word can always be trusted. So pain, sickness, confusion and death must come from the prince of lies, from the one who is here to steal, kill and destroy. Lord, my life is neither what I want it to be nor is it what I expected it to be. This is not your fault. But Lord, you say that if anyone should lack wisdom, he should ask for it. So Lord, right now, give me wisdom. Show me Your path for my life. In the name of Jesus, I reclaim my authority as head of my marriage. Lord, send your Holy Spirit to dwell in this place and in me. Remove any confusion and resentment that may be in my heart and mind so I can hear you speak to me clearly. Lead me, Lord, so I can lead my family. Teach me how to stand up when others faint. Embed your word in my heart so that when I speak to others, all they hear is Your Word. Also, Lord, I thank You for giving me the authority over my life again and for the immediate changes I will see.

In Jesus' mighty and righteous name,

Amen!

Prayer is POWER! Grace is POWER! Without these two, we have nothing. God gave them to Christians freely. He allows us to communicate with Him freely, and He sends us His grace and He says His grace is sufficient. This is a spiritual battle. You cannot fight a spiritual battle with fleshly weapons. You must use spiritual weapons and the greatest weapon is the word of God. Hebrews 4:12 says, "For the word of God is alive and active. Sharper than any double-edged sword, it penetrates even to dividing soul and spirit, joints and marrow; it judges the thoughts and attitudes of the heart."

So rise up, mighty men of valor! Grab your swords and read to learn, not to check off a box from a check list. Memorize God's word and know his promises for you. Then you will truly be a more effective weapon for the Kingdom of God today!

VALOR

Definition of VALOR (Merriam-Webster):

Strength of mind or spirit that enables a person to encounter danger with firmness: personal bravery.

Examples of VALOR:

- The soldiers received the nation's highest award for *valor.*

- The absence of indecision even in the face of death is the true mark of *valor>*

Origin of VALOR

Middle English *valour* worth, worthiness, bravery, from Anglo-French, from Medieval Latin *valor,* from Latin *valere* to be of worth, be strong

Related to VALOR

Synonyms: bottle [*British slang*], bravery, courageousness, daring, daringness, dauntlessness, doughtiness, fearlessness, gallantry, greatheartedness, guts, gutsiness, hardihood, heart, heroism, intestinal fortitude, intrepidity, intrepidness, moxie, nerve, pecker [*chiefly British*], prowess, stoutness, courage, virtue

Antonyms: cowardice, cowardliness, cravenness, dastardliness, poltroonery, spinelessness.

Judges 6:12 (NKJV)

And the Angel of the LORD appeared to him, and said to him, "The LORD *is* with you, you mighty man of valor!"

Joshua 10:7

So Joshua ascended from Gilgal, he and all the people of

war with him, and all the mighty men of valor.

The Standard Bearer

*V*ery few people today become surprised by the statement that traditional marriages are under attack. Compared to a marriage in the 1950's, today's traditional marriage is almost a 180 degree turn. It's no surprise to hear about people being on their second, third and sometimes fourth marriages or more. Spouses have become as disposable as diapers. We use them for their original purpose, but once they're full of "surprises" we trash them for a clean, brand new one. However, it is typically not the diaper's fault that it's messy.

A spouse will rarely say that he or she is the reason for the divorce. It's always the other person's fault. However, today we're not just facing an issue with divorce. We are fighting confusion on what marriage itself should look like. Is it between a man and a woman, or is it between "two people"? If the adults are confused, imagine how the children feel. As children growing up in today's society, who can blame them if they grow up thinking they never want to participate in marriage? After all, many children see nothing but fighting and problems. Why would they want to commit to something that is just a problem? Maybe that is why most young adults today live together without being married. They have the relationship without the commitment. If it doesn't work out, they just have to move, no "divorce" necessary.

A major problem in marriage today is that people don't look to the true standard. They only look to the worlds standard and the world says: "Follow your heart", "Do what feels right to you", and "Whatever makes you happy." The problem with this is that your heart will deceive you. This is what the LORD says in Jeremiah 17: 5-10 (NIV).

"Cursed is the one who trusts in man, who draws strength from mere flesh and whose heart turns away from the LORD. That person will be like a bush in the wastelands; they will not see prosperity when it comes. They will dwell in the parched places of the desert, in a salt land where no one lives. "But blessed is the one who trusts in the LORD, whose confidence is in him. They will be like a tree planted by the water that sends out its roots by the stream. It does not fear when heat comes; its leaves are always green. It has no worries in a year of drought and never fails to bear fruit." The heart is deceitful above all things and beyond cure. Who can understand it?[1] "I the LORD search the heart and examine the mind, to reward each person according to their conduct, according to what their deeds deserve."

The Bible says that following your heart will deceive you. Sometimes your heart will say to you, you need to find a new spouse or do not tell the store clerk you got too much change back. The world's standards change daily especially when it comes to what is good for you to eat and wear, how much to sleep, where to vacation and what to watch. In this context, following worldly "standards" seems pretty foolish.

However, to understand what standard to follow, we first must learn what a standard is. The Merriam-Webster Dictionary defines a standard as:

1. A conspicuous object (as a banner) formerly carried at the top of a pole and used to mark a rallying point especially in battle or to serve as an emblem.

2. A long narrow tapering flag that is personal to an individual or corporation and bears heraldic devices.

3. Something established by authority, custom or general consent as a model or example.

4. Something set up and established by authority as a rule for the measure of quantity, weight, extent, value or quality.

5. The fineness and legally fixed weight of the metal used in coins

6. A structure built for or serving as a base or support.

In times of war when soldiers marched onto the battlefield, they would look to the "standard" in front of them that was held up high for all the men to see. No matter how chaotic the battle became, the soldiers could always look up and see that the standard was moving forward. If the standard bearer was killed, another soldier would pick up the standard and keep it high. But the standard itself never changed. It was always constant and up high for everyone to see and follow.

If the standard fell and was not raised again, the remaining soldiers would retreat. Perhaps that is what has happened to men today. The standard has fallen and has not been lifted again so men have nothing to look to for leadership.

So let me ask: What or who do you follow? What is your standard? Is it constant and held high? Or is it always changing? In today's time, there are very few things that have remained unchanged. The only thing I know of that has stood the test of time without being changed is the Holy Bible. It is always constant because God's promises never change. Truth is always constant and will set you free! So make sure you're following the standard and not the standard bearer. The standard bearer (pastors, friends, relatives, religions) can fall at any time. If we are following them, we will go right over the cliff with them. If we are following the standard itself; however, it does not matter who is holding it up. It will remain unchanged.

Where are the men today?

I grew up thinking that the world was full of strongmen. The first strong man in my life was my father. He is a Vietnam veteran and is a retired DPS officer and a Texas Ranger. He worked hard for all we had, and even worked extra jobs so that we could have a few extras. Work was essential to provide necessities; however, work was never more important than his family. There was never a moment when he did not make time for us. He was the head of our house and he led his family to church every week. He took me fishing and played catch with me. He helped cook dinner and he helped with laundry. Yes, the whites did turn pink more often than not, but he never shirked his responsibilities as a husband and father. Together, we sat at the dinner table to eat as a family, and no one ate until dad prayed. There were no excuses for missing family dinner, and there was always enough food for any unexpected guests. When the weather was stormy, my house was the refuge for all the soaked, hungry neighborhood children.

But today's family is very different. Many families are split by divorce. Certainly there was divorce when I was growing up, even right across the street with the family of one of my best friends. Today, however, divorced families seem more common than families who are still together. Children are shared over weekends and holidays. If the parents are still married, many times dad is working late. Pizza is ordered and eaten on the go. Drive-thru windows serve cuisine to our families on their way to soccer, ballet and karate. Parents are more like chauffeurs than people with influence in their children's lives. The family schedule is so busy that in many cases, the parents don't even get to stay and watch the practice. The children's extracurricular schedule has them driving all evening taking and dropping off kids. In most cases, moms and dads both work which adds more time pressure to each evening especially if there is a requirement that keeps one of them late at the office or one parent called to go out of town for a few nights. Sometimes a husband must work in another city or even a different state during the week and come home on weekends, putting the wife and mother in the role of a single mom.

Because of these crazy schedules, many men look for an escape. They are often more interested in fantasyland than reality. They play fantasy baseball, fantasy football, Xbox, play stations, Nintendo Wii and online multiplayer games. They are more into diving in and surrounding themselves with a make-believe life than standing up and facing what's right in front of them: reality! There's nothing wrong with playing paintball with your buddies or a round of golf, or watching football on a Saturday or Sunday afternoon. When extracurricular activities prevent you from taking responsibility for your own life and the life of your family, however, there is a problem. When guys would rather go hunting on Thanksgiving Day with their pals rather than having a Thanksgiving dinner with their wives and family, priorities may be skewed.

Many men think when they get married, their wives will have to accept any decisions they make. After all, they are the "man" of the house. The Bible says that women should submit to their husbands. But it also says that husbands should love their wives as Christ loves the church. If you do not love your wife as Christ loves the Church, why should she respect you? Putting a ring on your wife's finger does not give you a license to hand your family over to her while you go and play games. Everyone needs a break from reality at times. Let's face it, life is not easy. Sometimes, life just stinks. We've all had a bad boss; we've all had a terrible job where we're overworked and underpaid. We all have financial struggles and have tough decisions to make. Even in difficult times, we are called to praise God always. We married our wives to spend our lives with them. Not to have children, and then take off to spend our lives with our buddies. Every man needs male friends. But these friends should not be men who tear down and take away, rather they should be men who add value to our lives and help us strengthen our family lives.

I love to go fishing. Now notice I didn't say I love to go catch fish. As much as I'd love to catch fish, it just doesn't happen too often. Some people have something called a "green thumb" where everything they touch grows. Some people have what's called the "Midas touch" where everything they touch turns to money or gold. Some people, every time they throw their line out in the water they reel in three fish on two hooks. I, however, can go and stand in the middle of a school of fish that have not eaten in five days, and the fish will find something wrong with my bait. Instead they will eat the bait of the guy standing next to me. Regardless of my fishing luck, I love to fish.

My wife and I recently had another baby; my wife gave birth to our fourth daughter. With a new baby in the house, this means I haven't been fishing in months. Thankfully, I don't have to go catch fish so my family can eat; I fish for recreation and enjoyment. However, fishing is not my only source of enjoyment. With my family, there is an environment that is very joyful for me. My wife respects me and my daughters are a blessing. They are still normal children, but they are obedient because they've been taught. So I find just as much joy playing with my girls in our backyard on the swing set as I do going fishing with friends. If my current circumstances are not right for me to leave my wife with four children, I just don't do it. If my friends bother me for not hanging out with them, I try to find new friends who value marriage more than they value the fishing calendar.

The biggest struggle in our lives is that we are all selfish. We all want things for ourselves. We look at situations, and we think "What can I get out of this?" How will this benefit me?" The problem with this thought process is that it is not how Christ lived his life. Christ came to serve, not to be served. When Jesus knelt down and began washing his disciple's feet, he was not thinking of himself. So why is it that we all struggle with the selfishness? The simple answer is that we are all sinners. There is nothing good in us without Christ. Sin began in the Garden when Adam and Eve fell and sin entered our lives. For this reason, we need Jesus Christ. And for this reason Jesus Christ hung on the cross and died. If we would all learn to live our lives not for ourselves but for others, we would realize how much joy there actually is in giving. If you have troubles, struggles or stress, the best way to alleviate them is to forget about your problems and serve someone else. One of the best places to start serving is in your own home.

Look for things that need to be done that no one likes to do. For example, my wife does most of the laundry in our home. When six people live under one roof and five of the six are female, there are some serious laundry piles. Occasionally, I will walk by our bed and see a pile of clean clothes stacked on top. If I am not doing something urgent, I stop and fold the clothes for us. It takes me five minutes, but my wife gives me so much praise for doing that small job to help her that you would think I had bought her some jewelry. I love to surprise her by helping with simple things. In the grand scheme of laundry, my five minutes of help is not that big a deal. To her, it's not about the laundry, but it's the fact that I saw the need and took time to help. She becomes joyful recognizing my love.

You know that feeling when someone makes themselves a sandwich and you see it and think, "Man that looks good. I think I want one too!" Then you realize there is another one on the counter designated for you. Judging by your excitement, that sandwich could have been a steak dinner. Remember that feeling you got? Someone actually thought about you and did something for you, and you didn't even ask for it. What a wonderful feeling, to be on someone else's mind. As my wife's late Grandmother Liz told us for marriage advice, "Always work daily at outdoing each other with kind deeds and words. This will keep your marriage fresh and new!"

Another example is when you run the dish washer before you go to bed. The next morning you wake up, reach to open the kitchen cabinet to get a coffee cup, but even before you open it, you remember that all the cups are in the dishwasher. You turn around and open the door to the washer and to your delight and amazement, it's empty. So you go back to the cabinet and find your favorite cup clean and sitting right there on the shelf. Someone came before you and emptied the washer for you so you'd have your cup ready and you didn't have to unload all the dishes to get it.

I think the ultimate selfless act was when Jesus said, "It is finished!" He took his last breath and died. He did nothing wrong. He did not deserve to die a sinner's death. We do. We are the ones who said those despicable things and thought those disgusting thoughts. We are the ones who lie, cheat and steal. We are the ones who deserve to hang on that cross. But Jesus said that by His stripes we are healed. He took our punishment so when God looks at us, he doesn't see our sins. He sees his Son, full of glory and honor.

So, I'm calling men to rise up. Forget about yourselves and think of others. Study and learn what Christ did and how He lived. Apply these thoughts, techniques and principles to your lives. This world needs real, true, strong men. Men who will take a stand for what is right not what is easy. The world needs men that will make choices based on the truth of the issue and not based on the popularity of the decision. The world needs men to rise up. This country needs it, our wives need it, and our children need it. If you grew up in a broken home, the best thing you can do for your children is to prevent a divorce from happening to your family by making a choice to rise up and be a man of valor. Make the tough decisions before you are forced to make them. A price will be paid. It will either be paid by you or your children. Sit down with your wife and decide that regardless of the struggles, and regardless of the obstacles, there is no such thing as divorce in your family. Jesus Christ did not come to make all new things; he came to make all things new. This isn't a call to go out and find a new wife or new life and expect God to bless that. Christ came to restore who you are and what you already have.

If you're facing a divorce, or unemployment, or if you're struggling with an addiction of alcohol or pornography, or any other struggle in your life, understand that Jesus Christ came to make all things new. So you have a chance to let those heavy chains of burden go. Give them to Him and He will set you free. Matthew 11:28 (NIV) says "Come to me, all you who are weary and burdened, and I will give you rest." Turn your thoughts and ways toward Him and He will put the pieces back together. Pick up the Bible and read about yourself. God has already written about you and your story between His pages. You just need to read and discover His way for your life. You should also start a praying relationship with God. You are His child, and He wants to hear from you. Just start to pray and you will begin to notice a difference in your circumstances. Your picture will go from a mess to a masterpiece in the hands of the Almighty. Author and speaker Lysa TerKeurst said (paraphrased), "The word Messiah begins with the letters 'mess'. So allow your mess to rest safely inside the Messiah and he will turn your mess into His message." Remember, Jesus came to set the captives free.

Stand Up!

*M*y wife and I had taken our children to the neighborhood swimming pool, where we ran into our good friend and neighbor, Steve. While we were wading in the pool watching our children splash and play together, Steve told me a story of an incident he just witnessed. One of the children at the pool, a boy about the age of eight or nine years old, had been running along the poolside when he slipped and fell landing on his knee scraping it a little. He noticed the look on the young boy's face, and also noticed that his knee had begun to bleed a little bit. Steve said the young boy began to cry and run again, but this time, towards his mother. Steve was in the water at the edge of the pool at the midway point between the boy and his mother. While the boy was running, Steve stopped him, pointed at the boy's knee with a little blood just oozing from the fresh scrape and said, "Ooh, cool! Blood! That's awesome, man!" The little boy glared at Steve with a puzzled look on his face as if he'd never heard blood being described as "cool". His expression then began to change from fear to a sense of pride. He began to feel that having a scraped bloody knee really was cool. He continued on his path running towards his mom; however, instead of running with tears in his eyes looking to be held and nurtured, he ran up to his mother and said," Look Mom, blood!."

Now clearly I don't know the history of this boy and neither did Steve. We don't know if this boy lived in a home without a father figure or whether his father was at work at the time. There is also no indication that says this father was doing a poor job of raising his son to be a strong young man. However, the boy seemed to be a little bit too old to be running to mommy for a simple scrape. I know there are many moms out there that would be aggravated with this comment and would say there's nothing wrong with the boy running to his mother when he's hurt. And I can't disagree with that to a point. Where does it end? When does the mother decide that it's time for the son to toughen up? At what point does a mom say, "Son, get tough." This usually doesn't happen. It is usually the father that makes a statement like that. It's usually the father that teaches the son about being tough and playing injured. Many times it's the dad that teaches a boy what a real injury is versus what is just a part of growing up.

But what if a son is growing up in a household of a single mother? And what if he's the only boy of the house with the mother and sisters? Where does he learn what it takes to be a man? Where does he test his strengths, especially if his father is not involved in his life? Or even worse, what if the boy does grow up in a home with married parents, but his dad is not involved in his life or his mother's because he's too busy with his own agenda? Unfortunately, this is an all too common problem today. Husbands and fathers are so busy with work and their softball league that they don't have time for their family. When the son asks his dad if they can go outside and play catch, the dad will respond with, "Not right now son. I'm busy." But what the child sees is his father sitting on the couch flipping through the channels or sitting at the computer staring into cyberspace or worse. And that's if the father is at home at all. Many men get so busy with work, they leave the house in the morning before the sun comes up and they come home after the sun goes down. They watch their children grow up horizontally. They come in at night when they get home from work and kiss their children good night after they're in bed. The next morning the dads get up early again and leave before the kids wake up.

The cycle continues. The children grow up with an absent father and moms raise their children with an absent husband. Children watch this happen as they grow up and think this is how life is supposed to be and they continue this cycle with their families.

Work is important. Men are called to be the providers for their family. We all need money, no question about it. Money is an important tool. But it is a tool, and that is it. What we do with money is what defines us. When we place the value of money higher than the value of our family and the relationship with our wife, however, our priorities are backwards and our house will not stand.

Now we have homes without fathers and without male representation. Our sons are being raised by mothers. Moms don't know what it's like to be male just like dads don't know what it is like to be female. Because of this, boys are being raised with the lack of a man's influence. They don't know when to be tough and persevere instead of running away and hiding or crying to someone. They don't know how to handle tough situations, so they avoid struggles all together. When an obstacle shows up, instead of figuring out how to get over it, they just choose a different path. They are put into baseball leagues where they don't keep score. Everyone gets to bat and everyone gets a trophy because they're all winners. There are no losers. This way, no one gets their feelings hurt.

The problem with this is it's not reality. It's not the real world. In the real world, there are winners and losers. When life gets tough and isn't going exactly how we planned, instead of communicating and working through problems, these men run and get a divorce or change jobs. They choose the easy way out. Men think, "I'll just go find a woman who understands me," as if it's always the woman's fault. What usually happens is they take their problems and personal issues and start a new relationship with a different woman, but their same problems and issues follow them. This will likely end the same way unless there is a self realization that the problem isn't with the woman. The real issue is with how the man thinks. Furthermore, divorce has become so common that society has accepted it as a normal part of life. It's not a big deal when people get divorced because it happens all the time. It's almost expected.

How many of us have been at a wedding and while the couple was saying their vows, we've thought in our minds, "I will give them 2 ½ years. Then they'll be divorced?" It is terrible, but that is how society thinks, isn't it? What if we thought differently about marriage? What if divorce were not quite as easy? What if there was a law that said that you are not allowed to divorce? If you did, you'd have to pay an absurd amount of money. Would that slow divorce down a little? Maybe, maybe not.

Two thousand years ago there was something called a covenant which was made between two people entering into an agreement. These people would stand in the town square before their peers as witnesses of the agreement. The two people would shake hands and proclaim their intentions for this covenant. After all, when someone spoke, that was their word, and their word was everything. Not so today. We say things and take them back. We have attorneys to argue about what a contract is and if it's legal and binding regardless of our original intentions. Lawyers sometimes try to change the definition of words. Former President Clinton got into some trouble, and he and his lawyers were trying to define what the word "is" really meant. This is absolutely ludicrous. When there is such uncertainty and people are not held responsible for their words, our very foundation is rocked. At this point everything that is built on top of this foundation has a huge chance of crumbling and falling down.

So men, when you stand in front of a pastor, minister, or Justice of the Peace at your wedding and pledge your vows to your wife, you should be held to these promises. After all, we all said, "till death do us part." Not, "till I find someone better, or I find someone who understands me better." It's time we take a stand, rise up and be held accountable. We should actually work at keeping these vows Holy. I know work is a "four letter" word in some houses, but anything that is worth something has a cost. Quit being so self-centered and man up! It's time that we take responsibility for our own actions and our own words. If we make a mistake, admit it and then make it right. It's time we take off our track shoes and quit running from issues and problems that we create. It's time to be an example to our children and teach them the right principles by which to live.

The Ripple Effect

*I*f we throw a pebble into a lake as smooth as glass, it creates a small splash that seems to disappear almost as fast as it erupted. However, it leaves behind ripples that travel from an initial state that can be followed outwards incrementally. The ripples travel out and away and theoretically, they never stop without meeting something of equal and opposite force. There are ripple effect examples used almost everywhere. An economic ripple effect happens when an individual's reduction in spending reduces the incomes of others and their ability to spend. There is also a ripple effect in our personal actions. If we eat at a restaurant and have a bad food server, we tell our friends about the negative experience. This usually results in fewer people dining at that restaurant which then leads to the need for fewer employees. Eventually, if there is not an interruption in this ripple, the restaurant will close resulting in higher unemployment. Unemployed people do not spend money in the free enterprise system which results in fewer sales and lower revenue for businesses. If this continues for too many businesses, you then have a downed economy. I know this may seem a little stretched, but you get the point.

Remember, what we do today will affect people indefinitely whether your action is good or bad. God calls this sowing and reaping. He says whatever we sow, so shall we reap. Bad seeds cannot be returned to us in a good crop. If we plant corn, we will not get wheat. If we plant a crop full of weeds, we will get a harvest full of weeds. Or plant a bountiful crop and we will get a bountiful harvest. So, I'll say it again. Galatians 6:7 (NKJV) says, "Do not be deceived. God is not mocked; for whatever a man sows, that he will also reap." Some people call it karma. I call it sowing since that's what God calls it.

I remember one time when I was in college. We always had study groups for organic chemistry at a local pancake shop. A typical college student never had much money, and coffee came with free refills. We had been sitting together and quizzing each other on the information that might be on the test the next day. A man came into the back room where we were sitting and sat at the table behind us. He was clearly not the cleanest or wealthiest man, which I could see by his clothing and the significantly unpleasant odor that lingered around him. He asked the waitress questions about the prices of every ala carte item, and was apparently trying to stay within a $4-5 budget. But we were focused and dedicated students and we carried on. As we wrapped up our session, I felt an urge to pay for that man's meal. I got up, found the waitress and asked her if I could pay for his food anonymously. After an odd look from her, she obliged and gave me his tab. I disappeared into the restroom for a minute since I had drunk seventeen pitchers of a mixture of coffee and half and half. When I came back, the man was gone. Some of the people in our group asked me where I had been and then proceeded to ask me if I had paid for his meal. I didn't want to say I did, but my answer did come out humbly. They then told the story of what happened.

The waitress approached the man and told him that an anonymous person had paid for his meal so he could leave without having to pay for anything. His response was quite unexpected. I had thought he would say something like, "Who was it? I'd like to thank them." Or, "Wow! I'm so appreciative." But instead he responded with, "*expletive* Yeah! Now I can buy more beer!"

My friends thought it was humorous and felt I had wasted my money on an alcoholic who could now buy more booze. What they didn't understand was the law of sowing and reaping. It did not matter to me what the man decided to do with his "extra" money. I knew that if I did what I was supposed to do because of the prompting of the Spirit, then God would be the one to hand out blessings. I wasn't looking for any accolades from my peers or from the man. I only do things for one reason: I do what God prompts me to do. We really will never know what that man did when he left. Maybe he did have a change of heart somewhere down the line and instead of buying booze, he bought some coffee and thought about some changes that he needed to make. That may be farfetched, but when God is involved, you never know what He will do. He does, after all, work in mysterious ways. Isaiah 55:8 says, "For My thoughts are not your thoughts, nor are your ways My ways, says the LORD."

Let us take this a step deeper. If I'm driving down the highway and there is a billboard advertising some "gentleman's club" with a risqué photo on it, and I choose not to look away, will that make a difference in my life? What if

I am eating lunch by myself in a crowded restaurant and the waitress is wearing a low cut shirt and drops something. As she bends over to pick up what she dropped, she shows more than she intends. If I choose to look a little too long or choose not to look away, is that bad? I mean, no one is affected by this, right?

I am at the office on a typical work day. I had an argument with my wife that morning and just left to go to work without resolving the issue. A female co-worker notices something is wrong and asks questions. I begin to spill how unappreciated and disrespected I felt that morning. She says she'll buy lunch that day. We go to grab some lunch at a quick burger place. There are a few other coworkers there too, but we grab our own table to speak privately so she can help me with my problems. There's nothing wrong with this either, right?

These actions all seem harmless. After all, there was no physical intimacy going on. I never had an affair with any of these women. You can't have an affair with a photograph and you can't have an affair with a coworker while eating a hamburger. Or, can you? There may have been no physical touching going on, but where was your mind? Were your thoughts pure and your intentions clean? Probably not.

Most people who have been involved in affairs will tell you that they did not intend for an affair to happen. They did not go into a relationship with the other person originally to have an affair. Their relationship just progressed and escalated. And now they're wondering how it got to that point and want to know what to do to repair the damage done. I have also read that most men who have affairs are happily married men with families. So how does this happen? How does a happily married man get involved in an adulterous relationship?

First, we must define what adultery means. Jesus said in the book of Matthew Chapter 5 that anyone who looks at a woman lustfully has already committed adultery with her in his heart. In this case, I don't know of many men who would be innocent of adultery. The question is how do we stop it? And even if we just look, will that look really affect our marriage?

Yes, adultery, even in the heart, does affect a marriage. A man is sowing seeds of lust when he looks at another woman regardless of whether it is on a billboard, in a magazine, on the internet, on television or in his office. These seeds will continue to grow. This harvest must be stopped.

My wife and I have chosen to home school our girls. I am not here to say that everyone should do this, but since it works for our family, that is what we have decided to do. However, we want to do this home schooling so we can teach them what we believe is vital for their education and future. Our first priority is to teach our children about God. We want them to know who their creator is intimately. We also need them to know about this country and how it was founded. We want them to know who founded this great country, at what price our freedom came to us, and what our founding fathers believed was vital to the survival of this great country. We are also very selective about what our children watch on television. They are limited on the time they can watch television, and they can only watch what we have approved. I will tell you, there is very little we approve of. At church, we make sure that the people who are teaching our girls and the children they associate with also lines up with the standards we teach every day.

We have been accused of keeping our children in a bubble and isolating them from the real world. My response to that is that we absolutely do. Why does society feel that an eight year old needs to know about all the immoral problems in the world or that a four year old needs to know about all the horrific crimes that took place in their city the night before. This is what is all over the news. So, we protect our children. That is what we are called to do. They will learn this someday. But for now, I try to keep their minds as pure as possible. My wife and I sat in on a conference where Ron Luce, author of *Re-Create: Building a culture in your home stronger than the culture destroying your kids*, was speaking about this very topic. He told us that it is our job as parents to preserve the innocence of our children for as long as possible. Let children be children, and don't force them to grow up so quickly.

When children grow up in a broken home, it's hard to keep their minds pure and unblemished. So many families go through divorce it is almost impossible to count the actual ripple effects that take place. A husband has an affair with a coworker and this leads to divorce. His children are young, but they still have ears. Children hear conversations the parents have that will last forever in their minds. Once the parents are separated and the divorce is final, the real difficulty begins. It is time for life to start over for the father and the mother. It is an altered state of a new reality.

Just like there are negative ripple effects, there can also be positive ones. It can be a simple random act of kindness like holding the door open for a mother carrying a baby and saying hello with a smile. Let's face it, when someone smiles at you, it is nearly impossible not to smile back. There begins a simple, yet mood-altering ripple effect.

How about when you are driving on the toll road? Have you ever had the experience of getting to the pay booth and the attendant tells you that the person ahead of you has already paid for you? Well, neither have I. However, I have been the one to pay an extra dollar for the unknown car behind me. If you have not done this, I highly suggest you do. Not only is it a good gesture of paying it forward, but it is an example of God giving us unmerited love. When the car gets to the booth to discover you paid for them, they may go to just about any length of trouble to chase you down to see who you are. It is a memorable experience to say the least.

One of the most difficult emotions in the human heart is offering forgiveness. When a person is wronged, there is a debt that must be paid. The offended has a choice. They can either shut off all communication with the offender, or they can choose to make things right and extend forgiveness. Once forgiveness is asked for, it is in the hands of the offended to either accept or reject the forgiveness. In reality, it is a struggle within the offended. There is a broken heart that tells them there is no way the forgiveness should be accepted. However, if this is the choice, then it is only the offended that suffers. Like I said, when someone is wronged, there is a debt that must be paid. There is no way around it. We must decide, as the offended party, who will pay that debt. Will we continue to punish the offender for their poor actions? I honestly believe the offended is the one who carries the weight of pain. Once the offender has asked for forgiveness, they usually feel better regardless of the acceptance.

If you are a Christian, you understand about forgiveness. Jesus hung on the cross and willingly gave His life for yours. By His blood, we are forgiven. So with this thought, when there is a debt to be paid, understand and grip the fact that Jesus has already paid that debt, and forgiveness can easily be granted even if it is never asked for in the first place.

Once you grant forgiveness to a person who does not deserve it, it creates a ripple effect for good. The offender experiences, first hand, the power of grace and forgiveness and understands how important it is to grant it to others. This creates a ripple effect of forgiveness. This world is full of hurting people. Remember, hurting people hurt people. When there is no forgiveness, there is no healing. But where there IS forgiveness, there also lives the Spirit of Christ.

So do you now understand the ripple effect of your choices today? Where will that ripple go and how far will it travel? When will you be revisited by that ripple and at what cost? There is never an end to the ripple effect of adultery.

So, knowing this, it is our responsibility to stop the ripple before it starts. Step up and be a Man of Valor. Look away when tempted. Stop going to restaurants where the waitresses wear clothing that is inappropriate. There are chicken wings even better at other places where you will not have to compromise your ethics and standards.

Obey: A four letter word

*M*ost wedding vows today do not contain the four letter word, OBEY! With such a rise in women's rights and liberalism, it is difficult for women to obey their husbands. After all, why should they have to obey him? What has he done that gave him authority over her? I understand that this word can be controversial to the way some women think. This obedience is not a license to push our wives around and show her who is boss. But the Bible has very direct instructions about who is head of the house.

Ephesians 5:22-33 starts with, "Wives, submit to your husband's as to the Lord. For the husband is the head of the wife as Christ is the head of the church, his body, of which he is the Savior. Now as the church submits to Christ, so also wives should submit to their husbands in everything."

Everything! It says that wives should submit to their husbands in everything. Yet, it does not stop there. It continues to say that husbands are to, "love your wives, just as Christ loved the church and gave himself up for her, to make her holy, cleansing her by the washing with water through the word, and to present her to himself as a radiant church, without stain or wrinkle or any other blemish, but holy and blameless. Husbands ought to love their wives as their own bodies. He who loves his wife loves himself... Each one of you also must love his wife as he loves himself, and the wife must respect her husband."

To present people as blameless is also to never condemn them or put them down publicly. It is to edify and uplift them publicly. Now, does that give it a clearer picture? Wives, respect your husbands. Honor them and submit to them. It is so easy to talk gossip with your girlfriends and chip away at your husbands by telling all the little dumb things he does. But this creates animosity between you and your husband. He does not feel respected and he will not honor you. Ladies, if you want to have a husband to live up to your expectations and be a real man, edify him in front of your girlfriends. Build him up. Do not lie about him, but find simple things and talk only good about him. Go on your social media site and brag about him. That may seem small and insignificant, but I can almost promise you that he will not make a liar out of you.

If you want a husband who plays with the children and changes the sheets on the bed, brag about how great a father he is and how he is such a wonderful help around the house. He will love the attention he gets, and he will find the task he has to do minimal compared to the praise he will get. Edify your husband! Build him up to be the man you want him to be. A wife has so much power in her tongue.

She has the power to build her husband up to be an incredible Superman, or to tear him down in only a few words to a pile of rubble. If you decide to tear him down, understand that he will not feel equipped to fight for you nor will he be capable to do so. He will think, "What's the use. She will just tear me down again."

Ladies, be in submission to your husbands. I understand that this is controversial, but before you throw your stiletto heels at me, first understand what the word submission means. "Sub" means under, in support of, foundation. Be in support of the mission of your marriage. You are the foundation of your marriage just above Christ. If you are the cracked part of the foundation, the structure cannot stand, and eventually, your marriage will fall. Be in support of the mission. Support your husband in all his crazy ideas, and eventually, he might have one good one, and you will be glad you did.

Men, too, must have a mission. Sit with your wife one evening and develop and write a family mission. My wife and I have done this. The Parks Family Mission is: "United and empowered by grace to be the city on the hill and the light in the darkness... everywhere we go!" So, everywhere we go and everything we do, we have this in mind, and we make sure our actions line up with our Family Mission. It should be typed up and placed it where it is visible in the home. The children should learn the Family Mission and recite it together as a family. The family can rally around this shared mission. It will create purpose and unity. Psalm 133 says, "Behold, how good and how pleasant it is for brethren to dwell together in unity! ... For there the LORD commanded the blessing—Life forevermore."

We must give our wives something to support, and I am not talking about the lazy boy chair. Get up, get out and find a mission. Build a business, raise your children, start a ministry, volunteer at your church, start a church. I don't care what it is, but do something. Pray for God to guide us. God has called us to be doers not consumers. Create things, do not just use up. God has given us a brain to use. We are limited on our productivity from our neck down, but from the neck up, we are unlimited. We may not always have two arms or two legs that work, but if we still have a brain, God can use that for His glory.

I know most people don't really do this anymore, but THINK! Since the addition of smart phones, we no longer need to memorize phone numbers or calendar events. So now we have all that extra defragmented space in our brains. Take thirty minutes a day, turn off the television, iPod, cell phone and computer, find a quiet spot somewhere where you get no interruptions and think! Sit quietly and allow God to speak to you. You'll be surprised how this begins to create some incredible things in your mind. But, I should warn you, as you start to think and listen to God, he will give you instructions. Once he does, he will expect you to obey

Him. James 4:17 (NIV) says, "If anyone then knows the good they ought to do and doesn't do it, it is sin for them."

In 1 Samuel 15, God gave very specific instruction to King Saul. God told him to "attack the Amalekites and totally destroy everything that belongs to them. Do not spare them; put to death men and women, children and infants, cattle and sheep, camels and donkeys." So what did King Saul do? He did this... kind of! He did follow God's instructions by putting some to death, except for Agag and the best of the sheep and cattle, the fat calves and lambs – everything that was good. These he was unwilling to destroy completely, but everything that was despised and weak he totally destroyed.

So did King Saul really obey God? No! 99% obedience is 100% disobedience. And because of King Saul's disobedience, the Lord came to Samuel and said he was grieved that He had made Saul king because he has turned away from the Lord and has not carried out the Lord's instructions.

When Saul was confronted with this, he said, "But I did obey the Lord. I went on the mission, Lord, you assigned me. I completely destroyed the Amalekites and brought back Agag their king. The soldiers took sheep and cattle from the plunder, the best of what was devoted to God, in order to sacrifice them to the Lord your God at Gilgal."

Here is what Samuel said back to Saul: "Does the Lord delight in burnt offerings and sacrifices as much as in obeying the voice of the Lord? So obedience is better than sacrifice, and to heed is better than the fat of rams. For rebellion is like the sin of divination, and arrogance like the evil of idolatry. Because you have rejected the word of the Lord, he has rejected you as King."

Disobedience was the downfall of Saul. He was brought down from being king of Israel to being tormented by spirits. But surely that would not happen to us today. God sent Jesus for us. He promised that if we believed in Jesus He would forgive our sins. This is true. But, does not God still call us to be obedient? If we really are children of God, should we not strive to be obedient to Him? In John 14:15 (NIV), Jesus says, "If you love me, you will obey what I command."

So, why would we not want to obey Jesus? It may be because obedience to Him goes against what the world says we should do. It goes against the world's standards which creates confusion. Once again, God says to flee from sexual immorality. But the world will tell you that there's nothing immoral about living with someone. There is nothing immoral about sex before marriage. And because of the confusion, our sinful natures say to go with what feels right. After all, God would not have created something as great as sex and told tell us not to partake of it. If people really knew how good sex was with our married spouse without sexual immorality, they would not choose to have sex until marriage. But, the world has perverted what good sex really is with things like pornographic movies and pictures.

Jesus said to obey His teachings, and there will be blessings that follow regardless of what we feel is right. John 14:16 describes this blessing: Jesus said, "I will ask the Father, and he will give you another Counselor to be with you forever - the Spirit of truth. The world cannot accept him, because it neither sees him nor knows him. But you know him, for he lives with you and will be in you... Whoever has my commands and obeys them, he is the one who loves me. He loves me will be loved by my father, and I too will love him and show myself to him."

How do we know if we truly love Jesus? We *obey* His commands! It is that simple. It does not mean we will be without sin. However, it does mean that when we fall short and sin, repent! We should try to stop falling into the same sin repeatedly! Repent from that sin, turn away from it, and move on!

If we are addicted to alcohol, we should stop associating with people who drink alcohol regularly. We should quit going to bars and stay away from the triggers that cause us to stumble. If we are addicted to pornography, we should disconnect our cable television and internet connection and cut off all forms of access to this visual, sexual sin. We should keep our computers out in the open where everyone in our homes can see what we see. Download software that sends emails to accountability partners telling them what websites you've visited. But no matter the offense, we must take immediate action to remain obedient to God's word. Once we do, the feeling of peace will overcome us and we will never want to leave it!

Escaping the World

*T*he book of James, Chapter One verse twenty-seven says the religion that God our Father accepts as pure and faultless is this: to look after orphans and widows in their distress and to keep oneself from being polluted by the world. It's interesting that throughout the entire Bible, this is what is considered to be pure and faultless. Taking care of widows and orphans seems pretty simple. Yet, that is what we are expected to do. Any person with the slightest ounce of human dignity would agree with this. This is revealed when there is a natural disaster.

When an earthquake of a 7.0 Mw magnitude rocked the tiny country of Haiti on January 12, 2010, 316,000 people died, 300,000 were injured and 1,000,000 became homeless. There were countless orphans and widows created by this catastrophic incident. The outpouring to this small country was overwhelming. People from all around the globe sent money, food, clothing, hygienic resources and even temporary shelters to help those who survived but were left with nothing. People who would typically not think twice about a tiny piece of land were suddenly digging into their pockets to lend any help they could. Catastrophe can affect any of us at any time. Wouldn't it be reassuring to know that if we were in severe need, there were millions of people willing to help even if they were barely able to do so? Helping out widows and orphans can be a simple process.

The hard part is actually doing it and not expecting someone else to do it. Our busy lives create many excuses for our shortcomings on helping others. One benefit of technology is it takes most of this excuse away. If people wanted to donate to the Haitian Relief Fund, all they needed to do was text to a designated number and they would be able to donate $5 at a time. Their cell phone company would include the amount on the next statement. Our human nature really only wants to help others as long as we are not completely inconvenienced.

For example, I would love to help my neighbor build a new fence. He is retired and the labor would take a toll physically on him if he did it alone. But, he chose a time for me that was really inconvenient. He picked Sunday after lunch right in the critical time of football season when the playoff teams were being decided, vital stuff that I really could not miss. No, I did not have anything invested in any of these games. And I certainly can't name more than three players, or even know if they are in the AFC or the NFC. But since I am a man, I must watch football. Surely this is a good excuse.

But what would I be missing really? Probably nothing that I could not pick up on a five minute blurb on the highlights. Plus, I wouldn't have to sit through the mindless commercials. If I had gone outside to help my neighbor, what would I have gained? Maybe nothing more than helping out a friend. Chances are, I would have had an opportunity to connect my life to someone else. Better yet, I could allow my life to be opened up to someone who has seen more life than I have. I might have a nugget or two of wisdom I could gain. In fact, my helping him with his fence, would probably allow me to actually reap the greatest benefit.

It is said too often that opportunities only come into our life once in a lifetime. I disagree with this. I believe that even if certain opportunities are missed, if you have eyes to see and ears to hear, God will send another opportunity your way. And probably another, and another. If we make ourselves receptive, we will be used time and time again to lift and encourage others as well as to add value to others lives. Isn't that what Christ did for us? He was sent to us not to just save us, but to add value to us.

The second statement in the faultless and pure religion in James Chapter One says to keep ourselves from being polluted by the world. This is an interesting statement. What is the standard to look to so we can make sure that we follow that which is not of the world? I'm guessing if we are reading the Bible regularly, we would use the Bible as the standard. Or would we? Clearly if we follow the world's standards, we will most definitely become worldly. But how many Christians do you know who have a Bible but don't really read it? They might know what some famous Scripture quotes are, like John 3:16, but do they really know what the Bible says about where your standards are to be set?

One challenge about the Bible is there are so many interpretations about what it really means. Author John

Bevere made a statement, "If we were to read the Word of God exactly as it is, most of us would be dramatically different from what we are." In reality, we don't want to take the Word as it is. We want to take the word of God and fit it and form it to match our lives instead of forming our lives around God's word. But what would our life look like if we took our life, trimmed off all the excess baggage, and formed our lives around what God says we need? What if we simplified things and only took on what God said we needed? We would be dramatically different.

The problem with this is the world says we need certain things to live a successful life. We must drive a certain car, live in a certain house in a certain neighborhood. Our children must attend a certain school and go to a certain church while wearing certain clothes. Society forms us into what it wants us to be. If we are not active in fighting this pressure on a daily basis, we will automatically lean toward living that way.

My family has chosen not to subscribe to any news-paper. When I was growing up, my parents paid for a daily news paper to be delivered to our house. I think they took it out of the cellophane package once or twice a week. The rest of the time, it would just pile up and make the house a mess. It drove me absolutely crazy because I was the one responsible for taking the recycling out to the garage. There was a stack of unread newspapers that were supposed to be opened, so I could stack them and tie them with a piece of twine so they could go to the recycling facility. It was more work for me to unwrap the papers and stack them than it was to bind them and stack them.

Years later, I learned that a fire broke out in my parents' house during the day while they were at work. The paper boy discovered the fire and began fighting it with a water hose after calling the fire department. If we're not for his water hose bravery, they would have lost the house. Since then, my parents resolved to always take the newspaper no matter what. When I was young, I did not understand why my parents continued to pay money for the newspaper. I wish they had just paid me the money they paid the newspaper company; that way I could have made some money and would not have had to stack the papers that had not been read. Maybe they subscribed to the paper for the same reason everyone else did: because that's just what people did. There was not much positive news in the newspaper worth reading; it was full of negative information written by some person I did not know with stuff I did not always believe. For this reason, I do not pay for a subscription to any newspaper. In fact, I cannot even remember ever reading a newspaper. I just cannot afford to have that negative information enter my mind; because once it is in there, I cannot delete it. Brains do not have a delete button to dump unwanted files, but wouldn't that be nice?

Ironically, if you had driven around my neighborhood when I was growing up, in the evening when it was dark, you would have notice a bluish glow in everyone's front room or bedrooms. Around ten o'clock in the evening most people were watching the evening news to see the local drama. The local news is absolutely appalling. Next to the national news, it is arguably the most negative source of information. It fills your mind with so much junk and, once again, you cannot delete it. It is stuck there forever. Pretty soon, you start believing some of that misinformation. You believe that the world will end in 2012 because the Mayan calendar said so.

I have not met any successful people who became successful by watching much television or reading many newspapers. I am not saying that there are not good articles in a newspaper. The problem is you have to weed through all the junk to find a decent article. No thank you.

One easy task we can do to fight the battle of becoming like the rest of the world is turning off our television and canceling our newspapers. But in the past ten years or so, a new enemy has hit our home, an enemy called the Internet. We all have it. It is on our computers, lap tops, iPads, smart phones and even connected to our televisions now. The Internet is everywhere. If you want to escape it, you must make a deliberate attempt to go far into a deep wilderness.

My wife is a native Texan, born and raised. Her parents are both from Ohio along with everyone in her family which pretty much makes me from Ohio. Most of them, with the exception of a few in-laws, are Cleveland Brown fans. And again, this pretty much makes me a Cleveland Brown fan. We were watching a Browns game on television and the game was not going quite the way we had hoped. When a commercial came on I somehow found interest and humor in it. There was a carload of guys in an off road SUV driving in the wilderness. The driver got out after coming to the edge of a cliff by a thick forest and held up his cell phone. He discovered he had no signal and said to his buddies, "Hey, this is the perfect spot!" They were apparently trying to escape the hustle and bustle of everyday life by getting to a place where they were unreachable. This took driving to a remote wilderness.

This is a sign of our times. We are always reachable. The Internet follows us everywhere. It is a good tool, but the problem with it is that it contains too much information. Most of the things posted on the Internet cannot be trusted. We must do significant research on the research we do on the Internet to determine if our facts are authentic and trustworthy. We have spam blocker, pop-up blocker, anti-virus software and even this isn't enough. The junk still gets to us.

In these days, just turning off the television and canceling newspapers are not enough to escape the world. It is a constant fight to keep our eyes clean, especially from lustful temptation and images. It is a constant fight to stay true to our call from Jesus when He said that anyone who looks at a woman lustfully has already committed adultery with her in his heart. With this command, it truly is not just a daily fight, but a moment by moment fight, especially when there are billboards up and down every highway advertising gentlemen clubs. I promise you, the men who go there are not gentlemen. They are men who are desperate for attention and willing to exploit that which was made to be kept between a husband and wife.

In order to keep ourselves from becoming like the world, we gird up and put on some armor. We are entering into a battle that is not of flesh and blood, but of the spirit. We cannot fight a battle of the spirit with fleshly weapons. We must arm ourselves with weapons of the spirit, the armor of God as described in Ephesians Chapter 6 verses 10-20 (NIV), "Finally, be strong in the Lord and in his mighty power. Put on the full armor of God, so that you can take your stand against the devil's schemes. For our struggle is not against flesh and blood, but against the rulers, against the authorities, against the powers of this dark world and against the spiritual forces of evil in the heavenly realms. Therefore, put on the full armor of God, so that when the day of evil comes, you may be able to stand your ground, and after you have done everything, to stand. Stand firm then, with the belt of truth buckled around your waist, with the breastplate of righteousness in place, and with your feet fitted with the readiness that comes from the gospel of peace. In addition to all this, take up the shield of faith, with which you can extinguish all the flaming arrows of the evil one. Take the helmet of salvation and the sword of the Spirit, which is the word of God. And pray in the Spirit on all occasions with all kinds of prayers and requests. With this in mind, be alert and always keep on praying for all the Lord's people. Pray also for me, that whenever I speak, words may be given me so that I will fearlessly make known the mystery of the gospel, for which I am an ambassador in chains. Pray that I may declare it fearlessly, as I should." We must sharpen our sword which is the word of God. This is our weapon.

We must renew our mind by washing it daily with the word of God. How can we fight an enemy we cannot see? We must read about the enemy from God's perspective. God tells us how He fights. He tells us that He is like a toothless lion. He tells us that the enemy is already defeated and that we have authority given to us by the power of the blood of Christ. How much confidence would you have going into a fight knowing you have already won but you still must fight?

God says the land is ours but He does not just hand it to us. In Numbers 13 - 14, God had the land ready for the Israelites to take. All they had to do was take it. Joshua and Caleb were the only two that believed God and remembered His promise to deliver them to the Promised Land. They were the only ones who, after seeing the land, had the confidence that they were able to overtake the giants with the help of Almighty God.

What about us? When difficulty falls on us, will we face the giant or will we run away? When life deals us a difficult diagnosis, how do we handle it? Will we have confidence like Joshua and Caleb or will we be like the other nameless cowards?

Now that we are armed, we must step out on faith and into battle. It is not enough to just believe God made us victorious. We must now go out and swing the word of God. Put it to use. Hebrews 4:12 says that the word of God is alive and active. Sharper than any double-edged sword, it penetrates even to dividing soul and spirit, joints and marrow; it judges the thoughts and attitudes of the heart. Just carrying the sword isn't enough; faith without works is dead. Use the word of God during an attack from the enemy to be victorious. God placed us on this earth and gave us authority over it. Because of this, He expects us to work. We are to work the land and take dominion. If we come up against an obstacle, we must take care of it. He has already armed and prepared us for this.

How do we use it? Here are some examples of how to use the sword of the Spirit. If we are under financial attack and pressure, remember that God will meet all our needs according to the riches of His glory in Christ Jesus (Philippians 4:19 NIV). So we shall speak this out loud to our bills. The word of God will not be returned void. If we feel an attack on our character or we feel that someone is out to hurt us, remember that no weapon forged against us will prevail, and we will refute every tongue that accuses you (Isaiah 54:17 NIV). If we are tempted by a woman, we can say aloud, "Get behind me, Satan! You are a stumbling block to me." (Matthew 16:23 NIV).

Just remember that there is power in the spoken word. An enemy can't hear what we are thinking; we must say things out loud. As we read the Bible, we discover things that come alive and speak directly to us and our personal situation. God's Word is a living Word.

To escape the world and not get caught up in it takes a radical approach. Friends may think we are a bit off our rockers. We may look different, and we may choose a path different from our current friends. But we must be willing to step up and make the change. Chances are there are others who feel the same as we do. They just are not as courageous and are waiting for someone to take the first step. Be willing to lead by example and from the front. Robert Frost said in his famous poem *The Road Not Taken*: "Two roads diverged in a wood, and I-- I took the one less traveled by, and that has made all the difference."Just remember, when life is over and we stand for judgment, we aren't standing in front of friends, but are standing in front of God Almighty. What words do you want to hear? I would like to hear, "Well done, good and faithful servant!" How about you?

Setting Boundaries

My wife and I started going to a church together before we were married. The pastor was fantastic, and we instantly fell in love with him. He had a gift for captivating an audience and unfolding a story before our eyes. He could open us up with laughter and then throw a bit of truth at us. Sometimes we would not even know what had hit us until it was too late. Sometimes his truth was painful, but we did not feel the pain as much because we were enjoying his company and his lesson. He was a normal guy, with flaws that he often shared with us. He never attempted to be a superhero and portray a perfect life. He was a husband and a father to a couple of children. His wife was even more magnetic than he was and had won our heart by the adoration she had for her husband.

I can remember a lesson he preached one particular Sunday about marriage. He was presenting an eight-week series about how to make a marriage last. What I enjoyed most was his lack of fear in talking about things that were typically not brought up in church. There was even a Sunday lesson coming up about sexual intimacy. Since he thought that subject would be too much for little ears, he warned us not to bring children to that service.

That sermon contained a good lesson. The pastor went into the details of how to keep proper intimacy with your spouse and I remember leaving there encouraged about my future with my wife. It was good to hear someone in a leadership role give marital advice about how to make a marriage last through temptations and also how to treat your spouse. Knowing that marriage was real and would last regardless of how Hollywood portrays it was refreshing.

A few years later, I received an alarming email which said there would be an emergency leadership meeting that evening at the church at 7:00. My wife and I were small group leaders and considered ourselves in leadership, so we attended. We arrived right at 7:00, and it was already standing room only. We should have arrived much earlier to get a good seat, but how could we have known? The email had not provided any information at all about the content of the meeting. The urgency of the message alone had intrigued us.

What we learned from the meeting that evening was that the pastor that had started our church many years ago in the living rooms of its members and had turned that church into a thriving three-service Sunday morning con-gregation, had been having an affair for the past few years with a church member. He was removed immediately and instructed not to return. That was the last we would see of him as a leader of the church. Of course my heart was crushed. This was a man who had stood in front of his congregation and taught about having an affair-proof marriage while he was in the middle of an affair himself-the nerve of people! How could he have done this? My only consolation was that God truly uses us for His glory, in spite of ourselves.

This church later relocated to a larger campus with a new senior pastor. It seemed to have survived the split. God was still working within that new church, helping it to thrive. Soon our family move on. We felt a prompting from God to seek a different church, one that would fit our growing spiritual needs. We later learned that the associate pastor from the original church had divorced. He and his wife had decided it would be better for them and their two children if their lives could be spent apart. They had been an active part of that church for many, many years.

When I heard this, I remembered a Sunday sermon preached by this pastor. He stood in front of that new gigantic church and taught how to set boundaries in a marriage. He described rules he would never break in order to ensure a long lasting marriage. He spoke of some great things. In fact, he spoke of things that I took notes on and still practice today. Yet, he is a divorced man with two children. No, a divorced pastor! Sadly, in a pastoral counseling class I recently took while pursuing my Masters Degree in Theology, I discovered this happens to 1 in 7 pastors during their career.

How is it that our pastors are teaching one thing but living another? Don't we all do this? We tell our kids, "Do as I say!" (not as I do). Right? I mean, we don't want our kids to follow us around all day taking notes because they would likely catch us doing the very things we tell them NOT to do. However, pastors are held to a higher standard by their congregations, and rightfully so. If they're going to stand up and preach one thing, shouldn't they be held accountable to it? Absolutely they should. Once they assume that role, they automatically lose the right called "privacy." People watch them at the grocery store to see how they treat the check-out person and the sacker, at restaurants to see if they leave a good enough tip. Preachers live in a glass house, without the privilege of throwing stones. People in leadership roles are expected to uphold a higher standard, well, everyone but the President of the United States. Surely he is allowed an occasional rendezvous in his oval office every once in a while, right? Wrong! Furthermore, if he will lie about that, he will lie about everything else.

One evening my wife and I were looking through our home movies to see what we wanted to watch. We decided that of the all the DVD's we had there was nothing that caught our interest. So I went to the local movie rental store to find the evening's entertainment. I came home with a few choice movies, one of which was supposed to be a scary one. It lived up to its genre; my wife was definitely scared. There was a particular scene where some kind of monster walked across the room with a broken up type of creepy movement. There came a time soon after for a break. While my wife was gone, I felt it appropriate to reenact that walking movement to spook my wife. Of course, this didn't go over too well, and it took all the persuasion I had to keep from sleeping on the couch that night!

After we had watched the movie, my wife and I both had the same feeling and thoughts, wondering why we had watched it in the first place. We were completely freaked out and felt terrible. That moment we decided that we would not watch another movie unless it made us feel better about ourselves when it was over. I know that the horror industry is big business, but that night we decided that it would no longer get our business.

We had set a boundary for our life together. We decided that our time and mental capacity were too precious to fill it with something that would invoke fear. We decided that we would only watch films that were encouraging, movies that inspired us to be productive and gave us the courage to chase our dreams and goals.

This was a simple boundary to set. We communicated with each other and chose to set a common goal to uphold that boundary to protect our marriage. Let me say that again! We recognized that there was an issue in our lives together that needed to be addressed. In this instance, there was a difference in movie appreciation. She was sensitive to certain films that I was not. We talked and together found a solution for that problem. We decided that our home would no longer host scary movies or movies that made us feel bad when they were over. We set a guideline to curb the problem. Now we communicate regularly to keep that boundary fresh so there is no way for the same problem to arise.

Of course, I like movies she would not like to watch, typically action and adventure films. She likes chick flicks and comedy. Regardless of the topic, when we watch together, I am sensitive to her needs and do not try to make her cross her boundary to watch something I like. I respect her boundary.

If a spouse will compromise in the little things, like not being more sensitive to the movies he watches, he will surely compromise on bigger issues. A movie is no big deal, but I still respect her needs and desires about what visual she puts in her mind.

One area in which I refuse to compromise is who I spend one-on-one time with. I will not spend any one-on-one time with another female who is not my wife. If I am at work and there is a female who needs to speak to me, I either have my office door open, or there is another female with me. I am never alone with another female. I do not ride in cars with just one other female unless there is a third person in the car. I do not have lunch with another female, even in a public restaurant when clearly there is nothing going on. I do not ever put myself in a position to be alone with another female unless it is my wife.

I know men have meetings and lunches with women often and typically, such behavior never results in any kind of adulterous relationship. Still there are a few reasons I live this way. I never want my wife to have the slightest doubt of my intentions or to think there is even the smallest chance that I might have been unfaithful. I do not want that seed of doubt planted in her mind. Second, I do not want someone I know or someone who knows my wife to see me and think there is something going on. Most people's minds immediately jump to the worst case scenario. I do not want anyone to see me, then call my wife and say, "I just saw your husband at a restaurant having lunch with another woman." This will cause gossip and, again, plant a seed of doubt in my wife's mind about my faithfulness to her. The devil can take such material and completely explode it in my wife's mind. Third, even if the odds are one in ten billion, affairs can start this way. That means there is one chance. I don't want to be that one.

In reality, most affairs do start this way. Two coworkers are headed to lunch break and to the same place so they decide to ride together to save gas and talk about how much of a jerk their boss is. Over lunch, she starts talking about her husband who is always playing softball and never home. He's always out with the guys and never spends time with her or her kids. The guy could talk about how his wife is always on the computer. She only fixes microwave dinners and is always tired. This relationship could be headed down the adulterous path very quickly. Typically, neither of them would know it. Pretty soon, it could go from lunch, to happy hour, to business trips and then full blown affair. Some affairs seem to begin with a simple ride together to grab a quick lunch or some scenario as innocent.

If you ask a recovering alcoholic who has been sober for several years how he did it, more than likely he will tell you that he changed his association. He removed the triggers in his life that would cause him to crave alcohol. He learned that if he was not tempted by the triggers he had a better chance of staying sober. If you remove yourself from the opportunity of having an affair from the beginning, chances are better you will stay faithful to your wife.

The problem is that the world tells you that there is nothing wrong with having female friends. Aren't we called to love and be kind to everyone? Of course we are. However, we are also called to protect ourselves from the enemy who comes to steal, kill and destroy. I do not have female friends that are not my wife's friends, too. I don't call other females socially. If there is information I need from another female, I include my wife in the conversation.

We have incredible neighbors a few houses down. They're a newly married couple with a young child. The husband had to travel out of town for work for several days if not weeks. We kept in touch with the wife and child regularly to see if there was anything they needed. One day I needed to borrow an attachment from them to vacuum our pool. Instead of running down to their house and asking her if I could borrow it, I texted her husband who was out of town, and asked him if I could borrow his vacuum. I already knew what his answer would be, but I wanted him to be involved in the process. I am always working on building trust with people. If I had just run to their house without asking him, it would have been no big deal, and he probably would not have thought much of it. However, how much trust did I gain by asking him and having him call his wife to say I was coming down to get the part? An insurmountable amount of trust! I gained trust with the husband, his wife and my wife. By taking an extra step and adding five minutes to the process, I gained a priceless amount of trust from my wife.

If we, as men, would work daily at building and earning trust from our wives, we could conquer anything. Our wives carry so much power in their words. With only a few words they can completely level us and cause us to be so unproductive it would take months to recover. However, they also have the power to speak into us and give us the power and strength to conquer mountains. The challenge is, to put them in the position to lift us up rather than tear us down. If our wives trust us, it is easy for them to edify and build us up. If they do not trust us, how excited are they going to be to send us out into the world of temptation?

Setting boundaries is not the same as setting boundaries or resolutions and then keeping them. A perfect example of the difficulty of this is a gym membership. The first week of January is the busiest week in a gym. By June, the gym is not so busy. Why? Action takes planning and commitment on a daily basis, and not just good intentions. Setting boundaries and resolutions also takes action and commitment on a daily basis. Our everyday lives of dwelling in the world can change a boundary. Work and friends push and stretch our boundaries. It is our responsibility to do a daily check on the pillars holding our boundaries up. If those pillars are bent, the boundary walls are lowered allowing compromise to flow in- one suggestion at a time.

One important question to ask is, "How do we know our pillars are bent?" There is only one way to determine if our structure is upright or compromised. We must compare it to God's word. If we are comparing ourselves to what the world says, there will always be change and compromise. For example, look at the simple example of an ever-changing topic – food. One day real butter is bad. The next day real butter is good, but margarine is bad. The third day they are all bad. A week later they are all good for you if they are ingested in moderation. Nothing the world tells you will ever stay constant. God's word, however, never changes and is timeless.

A few months ago I received an email that was full of advertisements from the old days. One of the ads said that more doctors smoked one type of cigarette than any other. So, people should buy this type of cigarette because that's what all the doctors were smoking in 1947. We all know that this information has changed, and now, not many doctors make smoking recommendations. Most people trust their doctor or at least trust most doctors in a general sense. After all, they are doctors so they must be correct. Two doctors rarely give the same diagnosis to the same patient. They always vary on what they think may be wrong. So if doctors' opinions are always changing, it's pretty safe to say that most other people are changing their views on life, as well.

When I was growing up, it was not common to hear of people living together until they were married, but by the time I got into high school, this became more common. Or at least I grew up and learned about that more. It became normal for people to date, then take it to the next level and move in together to see how that worked. If living together worked out, the couple would possibly get engaged a few years later. After a couple years of successful engagement, a marriage would happen. This is just how it was, and no one really criticized the behavior. Occasionally, you would hear an older person talk negatively about this way of living, but not much else would be said and the topic would be dropped. If an unmarried couple was living together, it was pretty safe to say there was premarital sex. If you were old enough to get an apartment or house and live together, surely you were old enough and mature enough to partake in the benefits of daily privacy, right? This just happened without the hassles of planning a long and expensive wed-ding. Who has time and money for that? So let's just skip that part and jump right into doing life together.

Now if a man has no standards or sets his standards according to a television show about a bunch of friends, this lifestyle of living with a woman without marriage will fit in perfectly. He will feel no pressure, and his life will feel normal. However, if he wants to set his standard according to what God says, he is doing things all wrong. This goes back to the ripple effect, as well. A significant other who leads to premarital sex that leads to living together outside of wedlock is all sinful activity according to God. Now I could sugarcoat it and not say sinful. I could say it is a frowned upon activity, or inappropriate behavior, or an alternative lifestyle. But, who are we trying to fool? I heard one time that the 11th commandment should be "Thou shalt not jiveth thyself"! You can lie to others, but you can't lie to yourself. Sin is sin in God's eyes. If it goes against His laws and word, it is sin. Living with another woman is not sinful. It is the act of premarital sex, fornication, that is the sin. 1 Corinthians 6:18 says to flee "sexual immorality" in the NIV. King James Version says to flee fornication. So, sexual relations with someone other than a man's wife is sin. And

God says to flee from this. By setting a standard on what God says, a man can determine if the pillar is holding up his boundaries or if they have fallen.

I know firsthand the damage of this lifestyle. My wife and I, through strange circumstances, chose to get an apartment together before we were married. We were both out of college and I was living at my parents' house when a tropical storm flooded us. Most of the house was damaged including all the floors. It was uninhabitable and I stayed with Kristen and her father. We had separate rooms but this started the trend of our living together which led us to the apartment before marriage. We got engaged to be married soon after moving in together. We were also engaged in sinful behavior that led to a pregnancy out of wedlock. We called ourselves Christians, but lived a life that was not following Christ's rules. We talked the talk and went to church on Sundays, but our lives were far from the standards God set for us.

The pain and humiliation of telling our parents we were expecting a baby was one of the hardest things I have ever done. I would never wish that pain on anyone. The shame I felt was unbearable. To make matters worse, I had forgotten that Christ bore the sin of my shame on that cross, so I carried it with me instead of letting it go. Unfortunately, the pregnancy ended with a miscarriage. We had no baby, but our scars were extremely real and very deep. We were married the same week as my wife's DNC procedure, a very painful experience both physically and emotionally for her. What was supposed to be the best night of our lives just continued to remind us of our sin. We were paying the price for our sinful actions.

For some time after our wedding night, our intimacy continued to be without the wonderfulness God promises a pure married couple. We continued to pay that price, and Kristen struggled greatly on an emotional level with the guilt of our actions.

I fear the greatest price we have yet to pay is for our children. One day, we will have to be honest with them about our lifestyle. We will not be able to lead by example. We will have to say to do as we say, not as we did. I fear this conversation and pray regularly for God to give me wisdom when this time comes. I would love to be able to tell my children that their parents stayed pure for their wedding day, but this will not be possible. We want our children to be on a path to purity for their future spouse. It would be even better if we could say that we were able to do it. We have many friends who have children who have remained pure and will do so until they're married. So we do have people they can relate to. How much more powerful would it have been if we were able to say we had done it, too.

Author Glenn T. Stanton wrote a book called *The Ring Makes All the Difference*, a book about the hidden consequences of cohabitation and the strong benefits of marriage. It is a must read if you are struggling with this issue or think it is not important. The facts stated in this book will help you understand why God says to flee from sexual impurity and sex without marriage.

I can tell you that my wife and I have been restored. Our wounds have healed from these actions; however, we will forever have the scars. If any couple has not gone down this path yet, do not! Get off this path immediately! It is wrong in the eyes of God and there is no other set of eyes that is more important.

One moment we may set our boundary walls to say, "It is wrong to look at a pornographic magazine or an x-rated film." Next we go to the mall and see a complete store window display of women dressed in practically nothing and think, "Well, that's ok, right? I mean, it is in public display, so surely, it's ok to look. They're just advertising clothing. How harmful can this be?" Instantly, our boundary wall has been pushed over.

So what can we do differently? How do we avoid the "pillar damage" that holds up our standards? Also, if there is damage, how do we fix it? There is a book called, *Every Man's Battle* by Stephen Arterburn, Fred Stoeker and Mike Yorkey, which talks about bouncing your eyes. You can't avoid looking at images most of the time. When a female crosses your path, you can't avoid looking at her or you may collide with her or fall into the mall water fountain. What you can control are two things: the amount of time you spend looking at her and the height or level of your eyes.

When you see this coming and you see the picture or person, bounce your eyes away and look at something else non-offensive. This takes a conscious effort and a great deal of practice. You see the offense. Quickly look away and don't look back. Don't return to the offensive visual, or you are guilty of lustful thoughts. If you see a female dressed inappropriately, pray for her. Pray for Christ to work in her life in a way so she will find her worth in Christ and not from the attention she gains from men.

If, in your peripheral vision, you notice a plunging neck line, practice discipline to keep from looking down past the woman's chin. It is possible. It just takes practice and discipline.

If I notice a female dressed in a way to steal my eyes and mind from my wife, I feel as though this woman has assaulted my wife because it is a physical and emotional feeling of pain and hurt to look at another woman in a way I should have saved for my wife only. If a man is not married, and does this, it is an assault on his future wife because now she has a standard set in his mind she must live up to on a daily basis. No matter how much she tries, his mind will always mold that lustful vision to be better than what is in front of him.

So men, pay attention to your wives. Look at your wife and complement her. Give her your attention. She is the one who deserves the stares, not a waitress serving up chicken wings. When you make a conscious effort to make it so obvious that you are giving her your attention and not wasting it on someone else, it will be very worth it to you! I promise! She will be more willing to give you attention back. What you will have now created is an atmosphere where you both are trying to out-do each other in a positive way. And there is never a better environment to produce a healthy marriage.

Power of Association

I think one of the most negative places on earth is the teachers' lounge. I have never heard of anything good, positive or productive that has resulted from frequently attending the teachers' lounge. My mother has been a language arts teacher and department head of a junior high for many years. My wife was a teacher for three years. During that short time, I lost more respect for the personal opinions of teachers than ever. At least when I was growing up, my mother did not come home and tell me all the horror stories that would be told in the lounge. But when my wife was attacked by an old dried up crabby teacher who should have retired forty years ago, I wanted to put that old woman next to Jimmy Hoffa. I had to defend my wife constantly, so she and I finally decided that her time would be better spent at home raising our new baby. We have not changed our minds since.

It is interesting what people will do when influenced by just a few other people. There is a video online of a lone dancer. It is a man dancing on a grassy hill at what appears to be an outdoor concert. His dance moves are quite entertaining and he is not shy or bashful about his ability (or inability) to move gracefully. At first, most people are watching him and laughing. After a minute, another man joins in and dances next to him. The second dancer is mocking the first but soon begins to find his own groove and dance like the first. Then a third joins in with the same mockery initially, followed by a pattern of dancing like the first dancer. Once the third dancer joins in, it gets inter-esting. A group of about five people join in to dance like the first dancer in his unusual dancing. Then critical mass hits. People are flocking to the small group of dancers. Before long, there is an entire mob of people where before just a simple lone dancer stood. Eventually, people became left out if they did not join in the fun.

We all want to fit in and belong, but very few of us are willing to be the lone dancer. Even fewer of us are willing to be the second dancer who steps in and validates the first. After all, almost everyone is laughing and pointing at the lone bad dancer. To be the person to step in and say, "Hey, this isn't all that bad!" is a big step, a step that risks our looking foolish as well. This is also a step that may be the one leading more to the pack.

Don't we all want to hang around people that accept us? Don't we all want just to fit in? Most people do not want to be noticed by too many others. They just want to be a part of something which, unfortunately, can lead to being a part of a destructive group rather than a constructive group.

However, destructive groups are not always that obvious. They are sometimes disguised as coworkers or teammates. They are sometimes people we are around five days a week yet only know on a work level rather than a personal level.

Let me introduce you to a friend named Bill. He is the typical, every day, single man. He is just working day to day without really having any major plan for his life. He has been out of high school for a few years and college is not really in his future. He begins working a new job. He finds he has a few things in common with his new co-workers-who invite him to lunch. A small group at lunch discuss gathering at another friends house later that weekend. Since Bill is the new guy, and he has been pretty easy going, the group invites him as well. With no other plans he decides to go to the party. When Bill arrives, he greets his coworkers and new friends. They offer him a drink and introduce him to a few other people. The night goes well, and Bill has a good time. Although growing somewhat late, Bill notices a group of his friends outside on the back porch and he decides to join them. The atmosphere here is different. Smoke floats upward as they pass around a single cigarette. He notices a smell strange to him, and he realizes that it is not plain tobacco, but marijuana. Bill has never tried it before and really is not interested, but he does not want to run away; they offer him some, and initially he declines. It circulates his way again, and they offer again. This time he decides to partake, so he does not seem like a prude.

Welcome to a new pathway. He has now joined a group of people who have started him down a pathway of destruction. His habit does not stop with marijuana. He tries other drugs including cocaine. Still, this all started with a simple gathering with some new friends.

A few years later, Bill marries and decides he doesn't want to continue this lifestyle anymore. His new wife is aware of it and encourages him to get out of that influence. The problem is he does not have any other friends. He has lived with this group so long that he has lost all his other friends. These guys are not bad; they are fun. They don't hurt other people. They just like to party and have a good time. Nothing wrong with that, right? Only there is something wrong with it. Drugs damaging effects are well known. However, Bill has developed serious addictions, not only with drugs, but also with friends.

Bill had become addicted to these people, but he had decided he wanted to be free from their influence. So he started hanging out with other people, his wife's brother and some of his friends. He starts doing things with them to avoid hanging out with his old friends. The challenge becomes continuing to work with those other guys. He sees them every day, and it is hard to keep his mind away from "the good old days." He decides to go hang out with them again for one night, which leads to three nights. Before he knows it, he is lying to his wife about where he has been and who he has been with because he knows she would not approve. To avoid a fight with his wife, he just does not go home. For some reason, in his drunken and high state, he thinks this is logical.

If Bill doesn't get away from the triggers that cause him to go back to a lifestyle he is trying to escape, it will be nearly impossible for him to break his addiction. He must cut all ties with the triggers that make him crave his addiction. If an alcoholic wants to quit drinking, he cannot go to bars or happy hour after work with his friends. Temptations remain strong and his will power is weak. He thinks that he will be able to be around alcohol but just will not partake. This rarely works because humans alone are weak individuals.

An addict who is trying to quit, must cut all ties that provide him with the addictive substance. If this happens to be with a life-long friend, so be it. If he is truly your friend, he would not be feeding your addiction. It might even be necessary to delete or block his number in your cell phone. Make it impossible to have any contact with this person or group of people. If you are coworkers with this person or group, ask to be transferred or to change departments. If nothing else works, it may even be necessary to quit that company and finding a different job. This may sound drastic, but it is not as drastic as your spending six months in jail for being caught in possession of a controlled substance and losing your job. Instead of your circumstances controlling you, you must control your circumstances.

I have a good friend who went through this very situation. The problem was that after his first stay in rehab, where he was away from his wife and newborn son, he did not change his circumstances. He left rehab and went right back to the old programs, old job with the same old friends who led him back to the same old habits of destruction. To no one's surprise, he fell back into his drug habit again. Before long he was staying out late after work and sometimes not even coming home. He was a nice guy with a newborn son, an older son, yet out running around doing things he should not because that's all he knew. He grew up in a home with a mother who would buy him alcohol while his friends thought he had the coolest mom. Unfortunately, she was leading him down a path of destruction and reinforcing this destruction at a young age.

There comes a time when we must all grow up and take responsibility for our own actions. We must decide that regardless of what happened to us growing up, we are not going to allow that same pattern to continue in our lives. For this man, it took another stay in a drug rehab facility. He did not get into any legal trouble, so he was free to come and go as he pleased. However, he recognized that he had such an addiction that he needed to stay the second time for a more extended period. His wife was supportive of his healing from this addiction. She was at home with their newborn daughter the second time. Although she was supportive, she was still in great pain and filled with anger about his selfish behavior. She remembered that she had said in her wedding vows that she would be with him in good times and in bad, and she stuck to her promise. Although difficult for all of them, when he came out of rehab, there was true repentance and remorse for his actions.

I sat down with this friend to have lunch one day, and to celebrate his eighth month of sobriety. I asked many questions about his experience and let him talk. He said the first time in rehab; he had not really been interested in quitting his addiction. He just wanted to know how to control it, so it was not so obvious and would not get him into so much trouble with his family. Once he was released, he had had surgery that required his taking pain medication. He then became addicted to pain medication, as well. He said that at the peak of his addiction, he was taking about thirty Vicodin a day. He could not think of anything else. He only thought of how he would need to schedule his day around his pill consumption. He was becoming creative with his bank account so his wife would not see the large sums of money being withdrawn. Then he went on a road trip with his wife, three children and his mother. Driving from Texas to California., he had to plan the entire trip, so he would have enough pain pills to last. In spite of his clever calculations, he did not plan carefully enough and ran out of pills. He told me that he actually began to go through detox symptoms while in the hotel. He was so sick that he had to spend an additional $3000 in plane tickets for him and his middle child to fly home because he was too sick to drive in a car. So while he was flying, his mother, wife, nine-year old son and newborn daughter were in a car driving across the country alone- all because he did not have enough pills. His wife was not com-pletely ignorant, but she did not realize just how bad his addiction really was. This was one of the defining moments when he realized it was time to get some serious help.

He said when he went back into rehab, this time was different. He really wanted help and did not want to live this way anymore. He was tired of having to live a lie every day.

He was tired of worrying about what lies he told yesterday, so he would not mess up his story for today. He was tired of this destructive cycle and really wanted out. He went back to the facility he left a year before, but the staff was not quite as friendly the second time. Although he was sick during the detoxification process, his sponsor would not give him any medication to curb the nausea and sickness. He wanted him to feel the full effects of his addiction so that hopefully he would never do drugs again. That is real tough love.

After completing this second rehab, he took the necessary steps for his life to be different. He quit his job with the friends who were supplying the addiction. He also deleted their names from his phone so there would be no temptation to call them during a moment of weakness. He began to surround himself with people who had the same kind of values he wanted. He placed his family around other families who valued the true strength and pureness of a family and who placed high standards on marriage. He started meeting with an accountability group which would keep track of his struggles and victories. He truly changed his association.

What does the Bible say about association? It is pretty clear in the New Testament about who and who not to hang out with. Here are a few passages about association:

Psalm 26:4

AMP: I do not sit with false persons, nor fellowship with pretenders

KJV: I have not sat with vain persons, neither will I go in with dissemblers.

NIV: I do not sit with the deceitful, nor do I associate with hypocrites

Proverbs 22:24

AMP: Make no friendships with a man given to anger, and with a wrathful man do not associate

KJV: Make no friendship with an angry man; and with a furious man thou shalt not go

NIV: Do not make friends with a hot-tempered person, do not associate with an easily angered

Romans 12:16

AMP: Live in harmony with one another; do not be haughty (snobbish, high-minded, exclusive), but readily adjust yourself to [people, things] and give yourselves to humble tasks. Never overestimate yourself or be wise in your own conceits.

KJV: Be of the same mind to toward another. Mind not high things, but condescend to men of low estate. Be not wise in your own conceits.

NIV: Live in harmony with one another. Do not be proud, but be willing to associate with people of low position. Do not be conceited.

1 Corinthians 5:9-11

AMP: [9]I wrote you in my [previous] letter not to associate [closely and habitually] with unchaste (impure) people-- [10]Not [meaning of course that you must] altogether shun the immoral people of this world, or the greedy graspers and cheats and thieves or idolaters, since otherwise you would need to get out of the world and human society altogether! [11]But now I write to you not to associate with anyone who bears the name of [Christian] brother if he is known to be guilty of immorality or greed, or is an idolater [whose soul is devoted to any object that usurps the place of God], or is a person with a foul tongue [railing, abusing, reviling, slandering], or is a drunkard or a swindler or a robber. [No] you must not so much as eat with such a person.

KJV: [9]I wrote unto you in an epistle not to company with fornicators: [10]Yet not altogether with the fornicators of this world, or with the covetous, or extortionist, or with idolaters; for then must ye needs go out of the world. [11]But now

I have written unto you not to keep company, if any man that is called a brother be a fornicator, or covetous, or an idolater, or a railer, or a drunkard, or an extortioner; with such an one no not to eat.

NIV: [9] I wrote to you in my letter not to associate with sexually immoral people— [10] not at all meaning the people of this world who are immoral, or the greedy and swindlers, or idolaters. In that case you would have to leave this world. [11] But now I am writing to you that you must not associate with anyone who claims to be a brother or sister[a] but is sexually immoral or greedy, an idolater or slanderer, a drunkard or swindler. Do not even eat with such people.

2 Thessalonians 3:14

AMP: [14]But if anyone [in the church] refuses to obey what we say in this letter, take note of that person and do not associate with him, so that he may be ashamed.

KJV: [14]And if any man obey not our word by this epistle, note that man, and have no company with him, that he may be ashamed.

NIV: [14] Take special note of anyone who does not obey our instruction in this letter. Do not associate with them, in order that they may feel ashamed.

Take another look at Romans 12:16. It does not say to hang out with angry men with quick tempers and with sexually immoral people. Do not be proud, do not be conceited. It says to live in harmony with one another and be willing to associate with people of low positions. Have we not all been in a low position at some time in our lives? Some of us more than once. And some of us have been in low places most of our lives. It does not mean we are bad angry people. It just means we have been in places where we would rather not stay. Garth Brooks has a song called "Friends in Low Places," a place of whiskey and beer. Not everyone's low place is there. Some of our low places are depression, for others they are financial devastation and bankruptcy.

When I was in college, I made extremely poor decisions about student loans and credit cards. I did not seek wise counsel about this. I lived in an apartment two miles from my parents. I was paying my living expenses on credit cards and with student loans. I did not have a job. Once I graduated, the funds from the student loans were all gone and I was working as a substitute teacher making $90 a day three or four days a week. That was hardly the financial return I was expecting. After all, I was a doctor with a $200,000 college education making $1400 a month at the most. I was about to get married to someone with zero debt while I was bringing on a Mt. Everest pile of debt. I was a 26 year old unlicensed doctor and broke. I was at my lowest place in life, filled with embarrassment and shame. I was so poor that I couldn't even afford to pay attention. I was that broke, and not just financially. I was broken spiritually, too. Even in my lowest place in life, I had people speak truth to me. My wife loved me for richer or poorer, and I was certainly poorer! The problem was I had sown so many rotten financial seeds that I was now reaping that harvest. I had no choice.

We are called to love our neighbor. We are called to associate with everyone who is not destructive. We are supposed to share the good news with all and never think we are more than a step away from a low place in life. But in all things, give thanks. When we are in our lowest place, the first thing we are called to do is rejoice! Sing praises to God. Even though we may be in a low place, we will get through. It always comes to pass (Isaiah 48:3 NIV). This too shall pass. As we pass through troubled waters, He will be with you (Isaiah 43:2).

Now take a look at 1 Corinthians 5:9-11. Here it says that you must not associate with anyone who claims to be a brother or sister (in Christ)[a] but is sexually immoral or greedy, an idolater or slanderer, a drunkard or swindler. Do not even eat with such people. I have had conversations with people about this verse and it has led to some strong arguments about who we are supposed to be friends with. Most of the conversations are with people who claim to be Christians, but do not have any fruit on the tree to prove it. They go to church a few times a year and may even have a Bible, but they do not read it. They just argue about small details in the Bible. They will pull verses out of context and argue that the Bible contradicts itself. But I have found that such people are doing this to justify their lifestyles. They want to take the Bible and mold it to fit their life instead of changing their life to fit around the truth and pure word of God.

One of the common debates is about who we are supposed to associate with. The Bible says that Jesus would frequently associate and stay with tax collectors and sinners. Jesus was always with the lowest of low. However, Jesus didn't associate with Zacchaeus, the tax collector, because he needed someone to hang out with. He wanted Zacchaeus to repent from his sins. The Son of Man came to seek and save the lost. Jesus never expected the sinners he associated with to stay where they were. He expected them to repent, to completely turn around and make right any wrongs they had made in the past. He did not want the gamblers to love him AND continue gambling. He wanted them to stop gambling and follow Him. In Matthew 4:19, Jesus said, "Follow me, and I will make you fishers of men." He did not expect the sinners he came in contact with to remain unchanged. He does not want people living a life of sin to love Him and continue to sin. He wants them to repent, turn away completely from their sin and sin no more. So if someone claims they are a Christian but are not following Christ's rules, then we are to treat them as stated in 1 Corinthians 5:9-11. It says that we are not even supposed to eat with these people. They are people claiming to be a Christ follower, yet they're living a life of sin. If someone is claiming to be a Christian, yet they're addicted to alcohol or drugs or watching porno-graphic movies, we are supposed to talk with them and help them get away from that lifestyle. Not out of anger or from a platform as if we are "perfect". God knows my life is far from perfect. However, we are to keep each other account-able. So if this person, after being confronted with their sin, continues to sin, the Bible says we are to cut them off from our association until they are left alone with their sin. Then God can work on them to become totally repentant. Then they are welcomed back to the association. It is difficult for us to know what to do in all situations like this. It is not an easy thing to do, especially with family or with friends. That is why it is so important to be in prayer before acting and speak with love to the person you need to confront. And the most important thing to do is speak with love, not con-demnation. Not one person is above another. Remember this and speak to each other with love and kindness. Put them above yourself. Serve them and find out how *you* can help *them*!

The problem with this is people do not want to expel the so called Christian who repeatedly sins with no remorse. Then there are no consequences for their repetitive sins. There are no consequences for the man who repeatedly cheats on his wife. No! We are called to "expel the wicked man from among us" (1 Corinthians 5:13). But the church today is too soft to do that. Most churches do not want to toss out a member. They need those numbers, and they need their tithe. So the church is afraid to hold people accountable to the word of God.

Now, with those who don't claim to be Christians, what do we do about their immoral behavior? Nothing! It is not our job to judge those outside the church. God will do that. We are just called to pray for their salvation and plant seeds into their lives by speaking *truth* in *love*. In the true salvation, they will be born a new creation, and all the old will be washed away. We are supposed to pray for the immoral brother, as well. If he is a Christian, we have more of a duty than just prayer. The phrase "tough love" comes to play here.

So who are we allowed to hang out with? Only perfect people? That is impossible. However, we are called to associate with people who are like-minded. We are all sinners and all fall short of the Glory of God. Choose one whose heart is pure and whose intentions are pure. We are to associate with them. Proverbs 27:17 says, "As iron sharpens iron, so one person sharpens another." Find people who make you want to be your best. Find people who bring out the best in you and whom you love and respect so much you do not want to disappoint. The best way to find someone like that is to be that person. You will attract what you are. So look around at your current associations. If you hang around a bunch of angry, negative people, you might want to do a check-up from and see if that is you, as well. If it is-change. One of the worst things you can wish on someone is that they never change. Like people said about you in your high school year book when they signed it at the end of the year, "Never Change! Always stay the same!" What a terrible thought. I hope in ten years I look back on my life now and say, "Man, I'm glad I've gained more wisdom and knowledge since those days." I pray that my association will continue to advance.

Cleaning out the Tackle

*A*s I mentioned before, I love to fish but I rarely catch anything worth bragging about. If I do happen to hook a good fish, it often falls off the hook the very instant I see what I have on the line.

Brandon is a good friend of mine who is a fantastic fisherman, a true angler. He knows the tides and studies the weather patterns. He knows the temperatures of the waters in Galveston Bay and surrounding fishing hot spots. Anyone can ask him a hypothetical fishing weather scenario, and he will tell him exactly where to go, how to fish for it (by boat or wading in the water), what tackle to use for bait, and what he might catch at what time. He is just absolutely amazing.

He told me one time that he was going to a weekend seminar on fishing in the Galveston area. I jabbed him in his ribs a little and poked fun a bit saying, "What? Don't you know what end of the hook is the sharp end?" He didn't think that was that funny, but I got a chuckle out of it. He began telling me how he was going to learn all the things I mentioned above. And he did! That proved to me that when a man wants to do something, he will. If a man tells me that he can't do something, typically he just does not want to do it. Otherwise, most men will find a way to do what they want to do.

Brandon and I have been talking about going fishing for a long time, but because of our hectic schedules, we just never made it happen. We finally made a solid date. I, of course, had to run out to the local fishing store to get a real fishing rod and reel; not one of the cheap ones that come in a combo pack with a superhero logo but a good rod and reel, so I would be able to keep up with Brandon. I had asked him some pointers about how to pick a good rod and reel, and I was happy with my choice.

The morning of our first fishing excursion was finally upon us. We met and drove down to the fishing spot, got out of the truck while it was still dark, and donned our wading gear. We were standing at the bed of the truck and he asked me to bring him my fishing tackle box, the one that I was going to take with me out in the water. I knew that when I was wade fishing I had better be sure that what I had in my tackle box was good because I would not go back to the truck once I had stepped out into the water.

I proudly secured the small clear hard plastic box that I just purchased at the sporting goods store. It fit perfectly at my chest between my shirt and waders so it stayed out of my hands and out of my way, but was easily accessible if I needed to change fishing lures. As I opened my case to display all of my neatly organized fishing tackle, I heard Brandon let out a long sigh. He looked at my tackle, looked at me, and said, "You don't catch much do you?" My first thought was, "How does he know?" Then I realized he was not being complimentary. He took one glance at what I thought was good tackle and instantly knew that I had no idea how to catch good fish. My response was, "Ummm…" That's about all I could muster.

So Brandon began to pick through my tackle box. He said as he tossed stuff out of the box and into the bed of his truck, "You don't need that, or that, or that. This is trash. What in the world is this for?" He practically emptied the entire contents of my tackle box except for the small knife and clippers to cut the string to change lures. He threw out all the lures I had brought. He tossed out all the swivels and quick-connect clasps, he tossed out all the hooks and plastic worms. He tossed everything out!

The thing I neglected to mention is I had filled this brand new tackle box with fishing tackle I had had in my old tackle box for years. In fact, some of the things I packed, I had received from my dad when I was young. They were so old they really should be placed in some kind of fishing tackle museum. I had never used them, and I thought I might get the chance that day. At least, until Brandon got a grip on them. I came to realize that all my equipment was old and worn out and useless. There was no way I was going to catch fish on tackle that was old, rusty and smelled like WD-40. If I did happen to hook something, the fish would probably either fall off since the hooks were worn, or it would break my line. I was trying to fish with gear that was completely of no use to anyone. And I had had no idea! It took someone from the outside with significant experience to dig through and show me that I was carrying around outdated and ineffective tools for the task I was attempting to conquer.

I felt completely humiliated, when Brandon finally said, "Here, let me go through my supplies and give you some new stuff." He then began to fill my tackle box with gear that was new and effective, telling me how to use what he was giving me and why it was going to work. I had never before experienced such good advice. No one had ever told me how to use any type of fishing lures or other fishing equipment. I had just tied the lures on and thrown them out. Because of my ignorance, I even had freshwater lures packed to catch saltwater fish, and I had no idea! This information was a real awakening!

We were finally all packed up when the sun began to peek up through the bay in the distance. We set out wading into the water and throwing out our lines to bring in prize fish. Out of about eight men who were all wade-fishing around us, I caught the first fish; a very large speckled trout. It was beautiful and by far the largest trout I had ever caught. I was so excited I could hardly breathe. Brandon was happy for me but did not share my total enthusiasm since he had been the one who had given me the right gear and showed me how to use it, which led to my catching one before him. In fact, I caught another one soon after that.

By this time, Brandon was reeling in his line and mumbling under his breath while he was changing the lure. He eventually caught up to me in the number of fish caught. I'm pretty sure he actually caught more than me, but I didn't care. We had had a great time. I was so excited. He had not caught a fish *for* me. He *taught* me how to fish for myself. He fully *empowered* me! Now I am still nowhere near the angler he is, but I am beginning to understand a little more about how to prepare for the next trip.

Strangely, I did not immediately embrace the magnitude of what I had learned, and I did not realize the depth of the wisdom I had gained from this trip. Only recently did I realize how Brandon had empowered me. I had been taught that that cluttered tackle box was just like so many of our lives. Many of us carry around old baggage. It is falling apart and useless. Sure, at one time, that baggage was new and beautiful and fulfilled our needs perfectly. However, time goes one and sometimes we need to learn to replace old tools with new, updated ones. The old tools are just dull and rusty. They may look nostalgic, but they really are just an ineffective reminder of our past.

Our church had recently challenged its congregation to participate in a twenty-one day fast. My wife, Kristen, and I had chosen to do the Daniel fast which consists of only eating live foods with whole grains and fresh fruits and vegetables without any animal products. We had about a week left in our 21-day fast so Kristen encouraged me to go fishing on a Saturday morning to see if God had another word for me. I jumped on the chance to go since it was a rare opportunity to be alone when I have four daughters all under the age of nine at home.

In order to leave before my girls woke up, I woke up at 5:30am and hit the water by 6:15am. The sun was just peeking up, and the sunrise was so glorious. In spite of the 40 mile-an-hour winds and arctic-like temperatures, it was marvelous. I settled in a cove where the choppy water was protected from the wind. I was not having any luck, and I really had not heard a word from God. I asked Him out loud to speak to me about what I needed to do next in my life. It seems like a broad question, but at that time it was very specific. Kristen and I were at a crossroads with our careers and lives. We were looking for the right direction.

God still had not sent any trophy-winning fish to bite the end of my line, so I walked up to an oyster reef to kneel down and replace my lure with a little more ease. As I knelt down, I heard God speak to me about the tackle box and how it had really impacted me. Funny how it took a physical act of submission toward the Lord, my kneeling down before Him, for Him to speak to me. He spoke, then, and I listened. This book took shape- a word not just for me, but for so many people.

Romans 12:2(AMP) Do not be conformed to this world (this age), [fashioned after and adapted to its external, superficial customs], but be transformed (changed) by the [entire] renewal of your mind [by its new ideals and its new attitude], so that you may prove [for yourselves] what is the good and acceptable and perfect will of God, even the thing which is good and acceptable and perfect [in His sight for you].

As I knelt down before God and listened to Him, I realized I had filled myself up with the world mixed with only a little bit from God. I had lived my life and collected so many useless things along the way keeping them stored up inside me. I allowed life to speak into me during specific times keeping what was said as if it were true.

The story in the Old Testament of David & Goliath illustrates this point further. David had a choice of what to put into his tackle box. He was small and with seven older brothers, he was easily overlooked. When Samuel went to Jesse to see which son the Lord had chosen, Samuel's first instinct was to choose the strongest and biggest son. But in 1 Samuel 16:7, the LORD said to Samuel, "Do not look at his appearance or at his physical stature because I have refused him. For *the LORD does* not *see* as man sees;[a] for man looks at the outward appearance, but the LORD looks at the heart." David was easily overlooked by many. It would have been easy for him to say to himself, "I am just a small nobody. I cannot make a difference. I might as well just stay out in the field and tend to the sheep." He did not do this. He knew God had a purpose for his life, that he mattered. He chose not to fill his tackle box with negative thoughts that would prevent him from fulfilling the purpose given to him by the Lord. He filled it, instead, with truths that came from the Lord.

David's task was herding sheep. He led them to food and water, as well as, protecting them from enemies. I can imagine during this time, he must have had some free time when he could practice with his slingshot. I can see him lining up some targets on the fence posts and taking a few shots at them with his sling shot while the sheep grazed. I can imagine the scenarios playing out in his mind as he launched each stone to crush the can off the post. Soon enough, unbeknownst to him, he would have the opportunity to put that sling to the real test. He would have the chance to quit fighting with simple bears, lions and wolves and have a real opponent - a giant named Goliath. In between the sling practice, he was told by his father to head to the front of the battle to take cheese and bread to his brothers who were soldiers. As David reached the front lines, he overheard the large giant making fun of his brothers and friends for being cowards and not wanting to fight. David realized that God had already promised them this land, and all they had to do was take it. He knew he already possessed what it would take to conqueror the giant. All he needed was God and trust. In fact, David responded by saying, "For who *is* this uncircumcised Philistine, that he should defy the armies of the living God?"(1Samuel 17:26 NKJV) David already knew the authority he had in God."You come to me with a sword, with a spear, and with a javelin. But I come to you in the name of the LORD of hosts, the God of the armies of Israel, whom you have defied. [46] This day the LORD will deliver you into my hand, and I will strike you and take your head from you. And this day I will give the carcasses of the camp of the Philistines to the birds of the air and the wild beasts of the earth, that all the earth may know that there is a God in Israel. [47] Then all this assembly shall know that the LORD does not save with sword and spear; for the battle *is* the LORD's, and He will give you into our hands." (1 Samuel 17:45-47 NKJV)

It appeared that most of the soldiers had forgotten God's promise. They allowed the obstacle in front of them to dictate their future instead of listening to God and remembering His promise to them. But there was one boy, David, who had favor in God's eyes. God had chosen this boy to become king since Saul had been disobedient to God. David was a warrior and knew God had his back! In fact, after he loaded his pouch with stones from the creek, he approached Goliath. No, he did not approach him, he ran at him. He knew what the assignment was and also what his reward would be. He had been promised great wealth from the king as well as his daughter's hand in marriage. On top of that, his father's family would be exempt from paying taxes in Israel. That sounded like a great deal. Interestingly enough, this offer was open to anyone willing to step up. Yet, only one boy trusted God enough to step out and take the offer.

What has God offered you to step out on a limb of faith? Has God called you out to perform a task? Has he planted a seed of an idea to start a business to bring Him glory? Do you feel called to change professions but are too afraid of what might happen if you do? Have you been called to write a book or song or learn an instrument? Are you called to adopt a child or be a foster parent or friend to someone in need? I have been in some of these situations, and I have also been disobedient in some of them. Do you know what God did to Saul when he was disobedient to him? God took everything away from him. He took Saul's crown away and in 1 Samuel 15:35, the Lord said he "was grieved that he made Saul king over Israel." In Chapter 16:14, it says, "the Spirit of the Lord had departed from Saul, and an evil spirit from the Lord tormented him."

I never want the Lord's Spirit to depart from me, much less have an evil spirit torment me. I would rather be obedient to what God tells me to do. In order to do that, it is important to know the difference between God's voice and the voice of something else. If what I am told by a voice does not line up with God's words, I will not follow it.

John 10: 2-5, 14-16 says: "The one who enters by the gate is the shepherd of the sheep. ³ The gatekeeper opens the gate for him, and the sheep listen to his voice. He calls his own sheep by name and leads them out. ⁴ When he has brought out all his own, he goes on ahead of them, and his sheep follow him because they know his voice. ⁵ But they will never follow a stranger; in fact, they will run away from him because they do not recognize a stranger's voice." ¹⁴ "I am the good shepherd; I know my sheep and my sheep know me— ¹⁵ just as the Father knows me and I know the Father—and I lay down my life for the sheep. ¹⁶ I have other sheep that are not of this sheep pen. I must bring them also. They too will listen to my voice, and there shall be one flock and one shepherd."

God loves his people. He wants you to know His voice and be able to hear his voice over all others. Isaiah 30:21 says, "Whether you turn to the right or to the left, your ears will hear a voice behind you, saying, This is the way; walk in it."

The Lord will guide our steps and lead us in the way to go. But we must remember to abide by His rules. If during our journey He says not to pick something up, that is for our own good, not His. We must not be trash collectors because trash will eventually push us away from the Lord. We can even develop so much pride we will eventually get to the point where we will say to ourselves, "Self, we are good. We will only call on God during emergencies. We have this thing called life licked!" What a dangerous place to be.

What have you placed in your tackle box that is taking the place of your wife and family? I know that some examples of popular occupants these days are television, sports, work, hunting buddies. None of these are really bad. Yet, if we allow them to take up more space in our box than they should, that becomes a problem. Instead of having a compartment for each of the above mentioned, make one compartment for all of them. We only have so much room in our tackle box. And we have two choices. We can spend our lives filling it up with things that will render us ineffective as Christians engaged in spiritual warfare, or we can keep it cleaned out and only fill it with specific items that will allow us to be victorious in the battles of spiritual warfare. Notice I did not ask if we were interested in engaging in warfare. We are already in warfare. The battles are constant. It is not of the flesh and blood, but of the spirit. (Ephesians 5:12 *paraphrased*) The battles happen all around us, like it or not. We can either be armed or unarmed. We must choose to pick up the weapons available, - God's words. Read them and understand how to use them. Know that we already have the weapons to win. Just like David, we must be the one to fill the sling and cast the stone at the enemy. He will fall if you take the time to practice. We must fill our tackle boxes with Scripture that is effective, and, hopefully, we will never lose a battle. There is nothing that can defeat truth. This is what Jesus is. "He is the way, the truth and the life." We must also remember that this requires our spending time with God daily and reading His words consistently on a daily basis.

Most importantly, we must pray! How can we have a relationship with a living God if we never talk to him? He is our Father; we are his children. He wants to hear from us. Talk to Him. Pray! Ask for help! His word says in James 1:5 "If any of you lack wisdom, you should ask God, who gives generously to all without finding fault, and it will be given to you. If you ask, it shall be given to you." Yet we must pray! He wants to hear from us. He wants to develop a relationship with us, not just when we need a huge favor or we want money; He wants all of us all the time. Matthew 11:28 says, "Come to me, all you who labor and are heavy laden, and I will give you rest."

Father of Mine

*M*y wife recently signed up for a ten mile race in Austin called the Austin 1020. It was a ten-mile race with twenty music bands placed every half mile along the course to encourage people as they ran. It was her first race longer than 5K. She has always enjoyed running, but never had the determination to race more than three miles until her brother invited her to run with him. She trained for few weeks and was ready to run ten miles in no time.

She told me that one of the bands was named Everclear; I remembered this name and recognized that it had been a band popular when I was in high school and in college. I could not remember what they sang. A few nights before the race we went on to YouTube to see what songs the band had made popular. Immediately, a song called "Father of Mine" popped up. We hit play to see if we recognized it, and we did, immediately. What we had not recognized years before was the hurt expressed in the lyrics. Here the lyrics:

Father of mine

tell me where have you been?

You know I just closed my eyes

my whole world disappeared

father of mine

take me back to the day

yeah, when I was still your golden boy

back before you went away

I remember blue skies walking the block

I loved it when you held me high, and love to hear you talk

you would take me to the movie

you would take me to the beach

you would take me to a place inside

so hard-to-reach

oh!

Father of mine

tell me where did you go?

Yeah, you had the world inside your hand

but you did not seem to know

father of mine

tell me what do you see?

When you look back at your wasted life

and you don't see me

I was 10 years old

doing all that I could

it wasn't easy for me to be a scared white boy

in a black neighborhood

sometimes you would send me a birthday card

with a five dollar bill

I never understood you then

and I guess I never will

My daddy gave me a name

then he just walked away

Wow! How many boys and men are out there, singing this song and claiming it as their own? Far too many are there to count! There is so much hurt in so many boys and men from what their fathers did, or didn't do. Too many did not stay around to be a daddy. They did not fulfill their duty to be there as a father. They said they would be there, but when things got tough, they were gone. It was easier to run than stay and fight. I don't mean fight WITH their wives; I mean fight FOR their wives.

The following statistics were found from a website called Dads4Kids.com. Overwhelming information on the statistics of fatherless children in America is easily accessible in an internet search.

- 63% of youth suicides are from fatherless homes (Source: U.S. D.H.H.S., Bureau of the Census).
- 90% of all homeless and runaway children are from fatherless homes.
- 85% of all children that exhibit behavioral disorders come from fatherless homes (Source: Center for Disease Control).
- 80% of rapists motivated with displaced anger come from fatherless homes (Source: Criminal Justice & Behavior, Vol 14, p. 403-26, 1978.).
- 71% of all high school dropouts come from fatherless homes (Source: National Principals Association Report on the State of High Schools.).
- 75% of all adolescent patients in chemical abuse centers come from fatherless homes (Source: Rainbows for all God`s Children.).

- 70% of juveniles in state-operated institutions come from fatherless homes (Source: U.S. Dept. of Justice, Special Report, Sept 1988).
- 85% of all youths sitting in prisons grew up in a fatherless home (Source: Fulton Co. Georgia jail populations, Texas Dept. of Corrections 1992).

For more statistics, please go to the addendum page.

Where have all these men gone? Why did they leave? Why did they not stay to begin with? When did men develop an idea that our wives are the enemy? When did some men adopt a thought process that their spouse was the one holding them back? When did we decide that if we were not where we expected to be in life by now, it was our spouse or children to blame, not ourselves? Why do men have to blame someone else? Remember, we are not fighting a physical battle. Ephesians 6:12 says, "For our struggle is not against flesh and blood, but against the rulers, against the authorities, against the powers of this dark world and against the spiritual forces of evil in the heavenly realms." If we are married, it is not just the two of us in our relationship. It is us plus angels and demons. There is a battle in the unseen fighting for and against us! The sooner we recognize this, the sooner we can gird up and put on the Armor of God. Not engaging in battle is, by default, being defeated in battle. This is kin to the same principle that says if a good person fails to help someone in need, he is guilty. If we witness a crime and do not report it or do something about it, we are guilty of being an accomplice. Recognize that Satan hates a marriage and does not want it to succeed. He hated Adam and Eve, and he hates us! He will do everything in his power to create division between my wife and me so we will not have children and raise them to be warriors for God's kingdom.

Author Dr. John Maxwell has written countless books on leadership. He teaches that everything rises and falls on leadership. If there is a problem with a major company, typically a change in leadership is necessary. When an explosion occurred in the Gulf of Mexico on an oil rig, the first question was, "Who is responsible?" And it is never the employee who is responsible, but it is always the person in charge. People are in leadership for several reasons. Someone must lead to achieve results. When things go wrong, and they always do, the leaders are always the ones on the hot seat.

So, who is the head of the household in Ephesians 5? The husband. When things go wrong in a family, who is responsible? The husband. I did not ask, "Who is to blame?" I asked, "Who is responsible?" Who is the one we go to when things go wrong? We go to the Father. We ask the Father for direction and guidance. We ask the Father for answers. We ask the Father to get us out of the predicament. The man of the house is the responsible one.

If the wife has an affair, is it fair to blame the husband? Is the husband responsible for his wife's actions? He may not be able to control her, nor should he have to. Is he responsible for his wife? A boss is responsible for his employee. A parent is responsible for his child. A baseball manager is responsible for his player. Is the husband not responsible for his wife? Genesis 2:23-24 (NIV) says, "The man said, 'This is now bone of my bones and flesh of my flesh; she shall be called woman, for she was taken out of man.' For this reason a man will leave his father and mother and be united to his wife, and they will become one flesh."

They shall become ONE FLESH! Therefore, he is she, and she is he. His actions affect her and her actions affect him. They are one. Since he is called to be the head of this one flesh, and the head controls the body, he is responsible to what happens to the body.

It is the responsibility of men to make sure our wives are fulfilled in every way. A fantastic book called "The Five Love Languages" by Gary Chapman goes into great detail about the five different languages each person can have. Every person has his or her own combination of languages, and typically, each spouse will have different language requirements.

Every person requires something different to fill their love tank. If their tank is not being filled by their spouse, it will eventually be filled by someone else, and this leads to adultery. The husband of an adulterous wife may not have spent enough time getting to know his wife. He did not know what her specific personal needs were. Then someone crossed her path who filled her emotional needs that her husband did not. She noticed that need being fulfilled, and she liked it. She went back for more and more. An affair begins.

Is it the husband's fault she chose to go back to the other man to have her tank filled by someone other than her husband? No. However, is the husband responsible for filling his wife's tank? Yes. Men are placed as head of our household which means all things within the walls of our marriage become our responsibility. This includes the well-being of our wives and children, physically and emotionally. We are the ones to fill our wife's love tank.

A wise man was once asked, "Sir, when should I tell my wife I love her?" The wise man answered, "Son, before someone else does!" When was the last time you brought your wife flowers or scheduled a surprise date? When did you go so far as to book babysitters and restaurant reservations? Before you were married, you did not expect her do to all the work on your relationship. You would go out of your way to woo her and spring surprises on her to make her think you were spontaneous and creative. What happened to that creativity? Was it all a lie? Or, are you just allowing yourself to be consumed by everything else that should be secondary to your wife's care?

Now that you're married, date her! She is worth it. Go on walks in the park and watch the sunset. Bring her flowers you picked from a field on your way home. Book a night away with no kids, and tell her to only bring her essentials. Then take her shopping for a new outfit to wear on your date that evening. Be spontaneous and creative. But most importantly, think and learn about your wife. Know what her favorite ice cream is or if she even likes ice cream. Remember her favorite flowers and bring them to her on occasion. Pay attention to little things. Write her short notes and put them on her car seat when you leave for work. That way when she leaves, she will see the note and know you're thinking of her. Just let her know you still notice her, and you are still in love with her.

People say that the magic of marriage goes away after a year or so. I say it only goes away when you stop pursuing your wife. Chase her, and let her know you are doing it! Fight every day for her affection. Fight to keep your attention on her, and her attention on you. My wife and I have been married over ten years. We are still on our honeymoon because every day we make a conscious effort to outdo one another.

We actively pursue one another, and we have so much fun doing it. There is no greater security for our children than for them so see us to affectionate with and to each other.

When we had our first daughter, one of our church pastors came to visit us in the hospital. As I stood holding that tiny baby and talking to the pastor, he looked at my wife and me and began to speak. As he did he began to poke me in the chest with his stiff index finger. He said, "Bub, the best thing you can do for your children is to love your wife unconditionally and out loud!" I will never forget that. For one reason, it left a bruise on my chest for a couple of days. More importantly, I knew the relationship he and his wife had and theirs was a marriage to model ours after. He and his wife were such an inspirational couple and had incredible children and now grandchildren. He spoke from experience and I decided to listen.

The best thing you can do for your children's emotional stability and security is to love your wife. Do so in such a way that there is no question how much you adore her and love her. Do it so often that it makes your little children say, "Ewwww! Stop hugging and kissing!" Those are the sweetest words from our girls because we know that they represent money in the bank of emotional security.

Come Together

*W*e've seen the statistics on what happens when husbands and wives divorce. We know how divorce affects children short term and long term. Anyone who tells you they are getting a divorce because they feel it is best for the children is making up terrible excuses to cover the sad truth. It is never better for children to have divorced parents. Parents' best choice is to grow up, and married, work through their differences by going to counseling with a certified counselor who believes in Biblical marriage. They can heal their wounds and become a living testimony of what kind of healing Jesus Christ can do. I know I am not a marriage counselor. That is why I said to go to counseling with a certified counselor who believes in Biblical marriage. I know it is not easy. Neither is divorce. In fact, divorce is guaranteed to be difficult forever. My wife and I are still working through the pains of the divorce her mom and dad went through when she was in middle school. Now our children are reaping the effects of that divorce. It is perpetual. So do not fall for the lie that divorce will be a good thing.

We have been married for over ten years, even though we have had problems and challenges. We are still married to each other because in the beginning we decided that there were a few things that would be constant; regardless of the obstacles we would face, we would never change these things.

The first constant in our marriage was that Jesus Christ would be our foundation. We would pursue him together as husband and wife. We would dedicate our marriage to Him and allow Christ to guide our steps. We would find a church that we both felt was our home. We would read Scripture, study it on a regular basis, and live our lives according to the Lord's plan, not the world's plan. That has not been easy. We are constantly checking with God's word to see which way we should go. Life has been very difficult at times. We have had to make some decisions for our marriage that made others upset with us. However, we promised to be obedient to God, not to other people.

Another constant in our marriage is the simple fact that divorce is never an option. From the very beginning, we burned the divorce bridge. We never bring up the word because divorce does not exist in our marriage language. This way, I never have to worry if I am coming home to an empty home after work; I never have to worry that she is going to run away with our children and leave me alone. That works both ways. She knows that I will stay dedicated to her and never leave her. I will not run off with someone else and leave her with no money and all the children to raise. She can rest assured that regardless of the troubled waters we are in, we will remain afloat. Isaiah 43:2 (GNT) says, "² When you pass through deep waters, I will be with you; your troubles will not overwhelm you. When you pass through fire, you will not be burned; the hard trials that come will not hurt you." We understand that God is our life-boat during the rough seas. We may sometimes feel seasick, but we know that God will not let us be overtaken by the waters as long as we stay focused on Him.

From the beginning, my wife and I have worked together on common goals. We have several businesses, and we work together on those. When we were first married, I worked as a doctor, and she worked as a school teacher. We left each morning and went off in different directions. We spent a great deal of time away from each other during the week as do most married couples. Not long after we were married, we started our own home based business. That allowed us to come together after work and communicate. We left our daily work behind and developed our business together in the evenings and on the weekends. We began to set goals and expectations together. We began to talk about what our roles would be and what to expect from each other. We then began to dream on a regular basis. At the time we were living in a one bedroom apartment. We would go out and look at houses we would only dream of owning. We would go look at Mercedes Benz dealerships and dream about owning a two-seater Mercedes Benz convertible specifically so that no children would be able to ride with my wife in car seats. She would get some private quiet time by herself with only the Texas breeze. We began to have hope where there had been little before.

Most importantly, we began to live life together rather than apart. Even though we would leave each other in the mornings, we would get together in the afternoon and evening and work to accomplish a common goal. We did not just come home from work, turn on the television, eat dinner while watching reruns of game shows and watch on through late night news. We did not come home and turn off our brains. Once we had left work to come home to each other, our day started. We stayed up late and associated with people who had the same dreams and encouraged us as we did them.

When my wife Kristen and I celebrated our tenth wedding anniversary, she posted a tribute to me on Facebook, listing the reasons she was in love with me. More than that, she actually posted ten ways to have a successful marriage. I want to share them with you.

1. Have a passion for Jesus
2. Dedicate yourself and your best to your family
3. Provide for each person in the family, whatever their needs and desires might be. (But keep this one at #3 and keep #2 at #2. Don't flip-flop them.)

4. Keep your priorities in line with God's standards.

5. Finish what you start.

6. Date your spouse. (Yes, I know you've already "got" her. This is how you "keep" her!)

7. Date your daughters, Dads! Teach them how they're suppose to be treated by real men and don't leave this up to teenage boys. (I promise they will teach your daughters incorrectly)It is never too early to start dating them.

8. Encourage your wife on her worst of days and cheer her on when she's having her best days.

9. Allow her room to make a mistake and never bring it up again. Ever!

10. Mentor other men to bless their wives the way you bless yours!

We learned very early on the power of positive thinking. We learned that if you want things to change, you have to change some things. If you always do what others do, you will have what they have. And if you do not want their lives, you had better do something different. We did not want a divorce to be in our future, so we decided to make friends and associate with people who value marriage and families. We chose to be selective about the people that we allowed around our children. We knew that once something was said, it was impossible to take it back. You cannot unring a bell. Our brains are like computers without a delete button. You can input all kinds of information. However, once it is in there, you cannot take it out. You cannot remove the negative; you can only dilute it with the positive. So we chose to read books and watch movies that made us feel better about ourselves and about life.

Ephesians 4:29 (NKJV) says, "[29] Let no corrupt word proceed out of your mouth, but what is good for necessary edification, that it may impart grace to the hearers." Another translation (NIV0 says, "[29] Do not let any unwholesome talk come out of your mouths, but only what is helpful for building others up according to their needs, that it may benefit those who listen." Be careful what you say. Make sure your words are uplifting and edifying. Your mother's old saying comes true here: If you don't have anything nice to say, don't say anything at all. This is so true. Your tongue has the power to build as well as to destroy. Proverbs 15:4 says, "A wholesome tongue is a tree of life. Use it to build and edify."

The words our wedding vows contained were powerful. They were words we spoke to each other and to God. We created a covenant with our words, a covenant with each other in the presence of God and witnesses. When we stood before those present, we fully intended to keep the vows. There was never an "unless" scripted in our wedding vows. So, we have a binding covenant. In Matthew 19 it says, "'For this reason a man shall leave his father and mother and be joined to his wife, and the two shall become one flesh[c]6 So then, they are no longer two but one flesh. Therefore what God has joined together, let not man separate." So, we were intended to stay together. Till death do us part.

Remember, your marriage is worth fighting for. Your wife is worth fighting for. Your children are worth fighting for. When you were young, it always felt great when someone stuck up for you. If you were in a bad predicament, was it not a great feeling when someone came to your rescue? Do this for your family. Movies like "Braveheart" and "Gladiator" are popular because a man took a stand against what was wrong. He finally said, "Enough!" and fought back. We all strive to be a William Wallace. We want a battle to fight, a beauty to rescue and an adventure to live, just like John Eldredge said in his book, <u>Wild at Heart</u>. We, as men, dream of these opportunities. We want to know that when they pop up, we will be man enough to step up to the challenge. The problem is we think it will be Edward Longshanks standing in front of us and our opponent will be easy to spot. However, it is not that simple.

Remember who your enemy is. 1 Peter 5:8-11 (NIV) says, "Be alert and of sober mind. Your enemy the devil prowls around like a roaring lion looking for someone to devour. Resist him, standing firm in the faith, because you know that the family of believers throughout the world is undergoing the same kind of sufferings. And the God of all grace, who called you to his eternal glory in Christ, after you have suffered a little while, will himself restore you and make you strong, firm and steadfast. To him be the power forever and ever. Amen."

Your enemy is not your wife, regardless of what your beer-drinking buddies might say. Your enemy is the devil, who thinks he is a roaring lion. He is not a lion. He is like a lion. He will work at you over and over again until he finds a weak spot in your armor. Then he will try to get a claw into you. His hand will break through. Next, he will get his whole arm into your armor and create a stronghold on you. Close up the defect in your armor now. That chink in your armor can be anything that separates you from Christ: cocaine, prescription medication that is abused, alcohol, pornography, gambling or physical abuse. Whatever it is, fix it. You must know who you are fighting. Remember the rest of the verse of 1 Peter 5. It says, "Resist him, standing firm in the faith, because you know that the family of believers throughout the world is undergoing the same kind of sufferings. And the God of all grace, who called you to his eternal glory in Christ, after you have suffered a little while, will himself restore you and make you strong, firm and steadfast. To him be the power forever and ever. Amen."

Remember, you are not alone. You plus Christ become a majority. The battle is a daily one, not one fought for a few days and then over. As soon as you take off your armor, you will be attacked. Stand strong! Galatians 6:9 (NIV) says, "[9] and let us not grow weary while doing good, for in due season we shall reap if we do not lose heart." The fight is worth it! The reward in the end is the crown! 2 Timothy 4: 7-8 (NIV) says, "[7] I have fought the good fight, I have finished the race, I have kept the faith. [8] Finally, there is laid up for me the crown of righteousness, which the Lord, the righteous Judge, will give to me on that Day, and not to me only but also to all who have loved His appearing."

It is not important how you started the race. What matters most is how you finish the race. If you fall, get back up because it is impossible to beat a fighter who refuses to stay down. We all fall down. It is our job as Christians not to kick fallen soldiers, but to help them back up, so they can continue to fight. You never know. One day, they may have your back and help you up off the canvas.

Again, it is not how you start, but how you finish this race called life. Just make sure you run this race so you finish strong. That way, when it is all over, you will hear the words every Christian aspires to hear: "Well done my good and faithful servant!"

Remember, being brave does not mean you are not afraid. Courage is not the absence of fear. It means that even though you may be afraid, you continue to move forward and do the right thing because it is the right thing to do. Our enemy is a paper tiger. He may look intimidating, but when you have the Word of God as your sword, any enemy can be defeated. Do not forget the definition of valor: Strength of mind or spirit that enables a person to encounter danger with firmness: personal bravery.

Personal bravery! When you walk with valor, you carry personal bravery if you walk with the armor of God and carry the Sword of the Spirit, which is the Word of God! With these things, all things are possible.

So What Now?

*L*ife is complicated. As couples travel this journey together, it is very easy to find yourself on a different path from your spouse, especially when you have different jobs in different parts of the city with your children all pulling at you in different directions.

It is easy to tell someone to work on a relationship. Without specific instructions, we often become frustrated and go back to the same problems. So to recommend a few new activities for your marriage, I have asked some close friends, whose relationships have impacted my wife and me, to send me their ideas on how they keep their marriages fresh and renewed. I am including the profession of each person to show that people from all professions and backgrounds must work to keep the newness in their relationships. Here are some simple and powerful ideas on how to keep your spouse the focus in your marriage.

Brandon and Tiffany - Age: 30's Married six years

Police Officer and Artist / Home Maker

1. We lead worship together (singing)

2. We have a daily devotional together

3. We pray together daily

4. Maintain a constant healthy sex life

5. We talk as much as possible

6. We have learned to communicate without words

7. we make sure we have date nights and weekends without kids

8. We make God the center of our marriage which connects us more closely

9. We surround ourselves with other Christian couples

10. Kids have a bedtime so we can have our time at night

Mike & Debbie - Married 40 years

Pastor& Grandparents

Debbie:

1. I love to cook and Mike loves to eat

2. I take care of the inside of the house and he takes care of the outside

3. We love to grill & talk

4. We have special deck time on a regular basis which includes a glass of wine

5. We have a special lunch date at the club every Friday and split the same dish every time

6. I love to take care of him and he loves to be taken care of

7. On a regular basis he brings in flowers from his gardens and puts them in a vase right in front of my kitchen sink.

8. We love our kids, grandkids, and dog and enjoy talking about them.

9. We have the same goals in life and love our Lord & Savior (probably should be #1 heehee)

10. We're on the same page with finances

Mike:

That pretty much covers it. She loves to watch cooking shows as much as I love to golf. WORKS for me!!!!!!!!

Matt & Kelly - Newlyweds & New Parents. Age 30's Hospital Administrator&Nurse / Director of Kidney Transplant

1. We sit on the porch weekend mornings and drink coffee together (I used to not be a coffee drinker... but I love drinking it with him)

2. We bring home small "sussys" for each other. Anything from a "love bug" purchased at a convenience store, to a cupcake from a nearby bakery, we try to keep it sweet with little nothings.

3. We relive our wedding on our anniversary and sometimes on other days too. We read the journal I kept with passages from each day of our honeymoon; we look at our photo album, and watch all of our videos that were filmed that day.

4. We make time for sex

5. We allow individual time. We understand we do not have to do everything together so we respect nights out or dinners alone with friends.

6. We kiss each other always 3 times before our heads hit the pillow each night. It is just our thing.

7. We respect each other during tough times. Our tiffs are few and far between, but when they do happen, there is no name calling, involving family or cursing. We handle our disagreements like adults and move on.

8. We take vacation together, just us.

9. We laugh with and at each other, sometimes just to be silly.

10. Now, we sit and play with Emily and talk about how wonderful it is that we created such a beautiful baby together.

Tom & Kathy - Grandparents & Married 40 years

Retired

1. We pray and worship together.

2. We go away together, at least one weekend a year.

3. We have a date night once a week.

4. We both have a sense of humor. This helps when things get tense.

5. We go for walks together.

6. We try always to put our spouse first, even above the children; our spouse will be there after the kids are gone.

7. We build each other up, instead of trying to change each other. We try to refrain from criticism, even if we think our way is better. Bite your tongue!

8. We stay connected with our friends. A night out with friends makes us forget why we were upset with each other before you went out.

9. We treat each other politely and with respect.

10. We say "I love you" every day and always kiss each other goodnight.

Lance & Juli - Age 30's

Finance Background& Real Estate Sales

1. We send each other random sweet texts!

2. He picks up the house without being asked!

3. We bring home sweet tea for the other!

4. He holds me in the middle of the night or in the early morning!

5. Attention!!! Lots of attention! :-) (Lance for Juli)

6. I push him to spend time with his friends whom he needs and he appreciates that I make him do these activities.

7. I push him to do more activities/volunteering

8. We watch and talk about sports together and truly enjoy it.

9. We consider each other equal; not one of us is solely responsible for anything...we are a team!

10. He lets me have my moments; when he sees me becoming stressed or overwhelmed, he steps in and takes care of whatever it is.

Tim & Michelle - Age 30's Married 9 years

Entrepreneur& Home Maker

1. We have a date night twice a month and don't let anything interrupt it.

2. We text or write notes to each other and try to keep that spontaneous.

3. I open the car door for my wife

4. We do chores and errands for one another, especially during the week, so weekends are more free.

5. We try to create private time for each other to enjoy hobbies, read a book, or be on Facebook.

6. We set time, once or twice a month, for deeper conversations or to address bigger issues.

7. We watch UFC together.

Nick &Lizz - Age: 20/30'sMarried 8 years

Aerospace Machinist &Director of Alternative High School

1. We pray together often.

2. We play softball together on a team. There's a rush we get when one of us makes a good play and we get pumped for the other. There's nothing cooler than to high five your husband or wife, all sweaty and dirty!! On the flip side, we can pick each other more easily or more quickly than others can.

3. Nick asks that I be in charge of the laundry because he doesn't like doing it. In fact, he loathes it. Works out well because I love it!

4. We have intimate moments or evenings with a spiritual and physical connection!

5. I am a big fan of physical touch and touch/caress him as much as possible. It is soothing for the both of us.

6. We do things for each other, like cook dinner, if the other one is tired or had a rough day at work. With

both of us working, we sometimes need to collaborate on job responsibilities at home.

7. We have family movie/game nights.

8. We praise each other: alone, in front of/ to our son, in front of/to our parents, and publicly (on Facebook, in front of others)

9. I take care of the house so he can enjoy coming home and be proud of his home.

10. Date nights are a must!

11. We admit our weakness and faults. Not be afraid to share our concerns, fears, distractions. It reminds us we are two broken sinners who can only place our full trust in God.

12. We cuddle, hug, kiss many, many times during the day!!

13. We show affection in front of our son. We love it, of course, but it does SO much for him to see that and know how much we love each other!!

Curtis & Juliette - Age: 30/40'sMarried 15 years

Nurse & Home school Teacher - Parents of 4

1. Every night after kids are in bed we spend time talking to each other

2. We have date nights

3. We work on projects together

4. We spend time discussing each other's goals and dreams as individuals and also as family

5. We play together

6. We disconnect from technology for a set amount of time, and talk to each other directly not via FB or txt or email. We look into each other's eyes. :)

7. Giving each other separate time usually allows for individual thinking. We then come back together with renewed focus and share with each other.

8. We have very similar interests and we genuinely just like to be with each other. We are each other's best friends!

Patrick & Kayla - Age: 30's Married 3 years
Logistics Team Leader & Delivery Nurse, Neonatal ICU

It was lust at first sight, infatuation at first outing, and love soon after, starting in October 2005. We devoted our lives to each other before God in September of 2008.

People say marriage is hard work. There could be some truth to that, but we firmly believe if you marry the right person, that hard work could be more accurately described as fun. It is extremely fulfilling to know the person you love is happy, and filling someone else's life with joy is nothing less than rewarding.

1. We touch each other, a lot. Whether it's holding hands, playing footsie under the covers, or playful tickles, the power of touch shouldn't be underestimated.

2. We thank each other constantly for doing even the most ordinary of things. *"Thank you for taking out the trash." "Thanks for loving me." "Thanks for being so awesome."* Feeling appreciated has a way of making life worth living.

3. We give each other compliments often. Just knowing your partner thinks you are sexy is one thing, but hearing it is almost flattering enough to count as foreplay.

4. We play instruments, sing songs together, and have lots of concert dates. Music has a way of bonding souls.

5. We give each other permission to be ourselves, moody days, gassy days, sloppy days and the best

of days. We know that feeling comfortable enough to hold nothing back just brings us closer.

6. We sweat together, soaking in some vitamin D and releasing endorphins; it's a powerful trio.

7. We kiss and hug often. Sweet, sexy, long or short, we do it, because intimacy feels wonderful.

8. We surprise each other with little gifts. The element of surprise keeps things exciting.

9. We keep it cheesy by writing to each other. Sneaky little "I love you" notes, cutsie poems on a facebook wall, a thank you letter in disguise as a blog post, and cleverly short emails. We keep them coming, documenting our favorite ones in a book at the end of the year, to read for a smile.

10. We are quick to forgive and short to hold grudges. No one is perfect. It is far better to listen, learn, and laugh together, than to form frown wrinkles and have tension headaches.

11. Each of us tries to always put the other first. Feeling taken care of emotionally and physically, down to the simplest of acts, such as getting out two plates for dinner instead of one, feels royal, safe, and loved, reaching that layer of the mind that yearns to be nurtured.

12. We never stop seeking to know each other better. We ask the other how their day was, and go beyond. We talk about everything, deep and shallow, enjoying the mission of learning new things about the other.

13. Each of us often tells the other how proud we are of them. Receiving positive feedback and feeling supported by your spouse can give you the confidence to excel and succeed in the world.

None of these things are particularly difficult, or take a great deal of complex thought, but they are all the little quirks in a relationship that combine to form a beautiful, exquisite privilege in this world, of long lasting love.

Mike &Kenzie - Age: 30/40'sMarried 3 years

Inner City Ministry & Outreach

1. We give light touches throughout the day

2. We unplug (turning off phones, TV, etc.)

3. We minister together

4. We go to lunches and dinners (without our phones)

5. We spending time traveling and time in nature

6. We give unexpected expressions of love

7. We take time to make each other feel special

8. We have surprise dates

9. We are reading Pilgrim's Progress with our son

10. We pray together

Tony & Marianne - Age: 50's Married 28 years with 3 daughters

Longshore Sales & Physical Ed. Coach/Pastor

Tony's List:

1. We have a morning devotional time together, along with our meal when we also review the day's schedule.

2. We serve in church side by side on the prayer team.

3. We are ready and capable of praying for our friends or in whatever circumstance arises, especially when driving.

4. Have a family meal time together, at least as much as possible.

5. We support each other in our ministry/teaching/ outreach activities.

6. We are open in our communications and being able to express our feelings without frustration or judgment.

7. We include our daughters in planning activities as a family when those times come.

8. We show affection for each other in public and especially when in family situations.

9. We work together to get our house in order and to try to keep it as efficient as possible.

10. We connect in knowing when to say "no" to the things that we do not need to be involved in.

Marianne's List

1. At the breakfast table we discuss 90% of life.

2. We have impromptu prayer where we pray for a need on the phone or standing in the doorway as

we are leaving. When it's our personal need, God blesses our hearts for one another deeply.

3. We have continuous communication and prayer through email and texts throughout most days,

4. We stand side by side in ministry: altar prayer ministry, mission, family

5. We share secret and random intimate rendezvous.

6. We have driving dates where we escape in Tweety(Our yellow Corvette) and drive until we find a restaurant or event or beach or hillside on which to hang out.

7. We have household chores which have become our own ....I do the laundry and finances. He does the car repairs, yard and makes the bed in the morning! This one little bed making chore blesses me in ways you can't imagine. A made bed brings peace to my soul which craves order. On a busy day when I walk into the bedroom and see a smoothly made bed,

the weight of the world is lessened and I am at peace.

8. Cooking: it's the one project that we do together that is easy with no conflict.

George & Tiffany - 30's Married 5 years

Industrial Worker & Hair Stylist

1. We go to church together. George knows that his staying close to the Lord keeps my love tank full.

2. We hang around healthy marriages! We learn how they work and we use their tools.

3. We try for quality family time!

4. We have weekend getaways as well as date nights:

    • Date night is fun and important but there are still distractions (babysitter/kids ok, curfew to relieve the sitter, etc...)

- Small getaways are completely different and required for our marriage! We go every other year! One year a vacation for the kids and the next for us! When I am away with my husband and everything is arranged perfectly back home for the kids, it is indescribable. I feel like a kid in a candy store with a cute boy! When I take these trips, I fall in love over and over again! There is non-stop affection and talks with no interruption! It's amazing and a must! I should write a book on this...

5. Intimacy!

6. The small stuff like notes, texts to each other, kisses goodbye while sleeping, facebook posts and compliments to each other.

7. We live in a completely honest household now! When you live with an addict, they live a complete

lie! They are taught in recovery to tell the complete truth!

8. We kiss each other first before we kiss our children. And we kiss in front of our children so the know we're in love! Always kiss goodnight!

9. We know everything about each other- from our favorite color to what we eat at every fast food restaurant!

10. We allow each other space! I need girl time! He needs man time!

11. If the other is not working we are together 99% of the time

12. We spoil each other completely! George is great at this! I require this but not material things! He is a romancer !!!!

13. We listen to each other.

14. We work well together and become a great team!

15. We make real cute babies!

16. George would change his whole life for me which proves he loves me that much! He stays sober, holds a good job, quit smoking, quit cursing and learned to raise our children better!

17. No jealousy ever!

18. Laughter! We joke.

19. We do not fight about money!

20. We truly honor our vows!

21. Did I say we make cute babies????

Charlie & Julie (Age 30's Married ? Years)

Chemical Operator & Corporate Accountant

1. I leave a note, email or text message for my husband every day, something to encourage him, to thank him for something he did recently, or just to tell him how and why I love and adore him so much. Sometimes he leaves me one, too, and it makes me

realize how special getting something like this every day must make him feel! This was my husband's special request for me to do for him.

2. We say a prayer together once a day (we take turns). This was my wife's special request for me to do for her.

3. Make time to spend with just the two of us - get a babysitter to go out on a date, talk/visit in the backyard, have movie night or go out of town, stay at a hotel, we talk about our lives together and not just about the kids.

4. Every so often surprise each other with something - an unknown date night, a present etc.

5. One more that REALLY helps is to be supportive and encourage each other to go spend time with friends or just yourself without the kids or your spouse. Continue to have a life outside of being a mom and dad as well as a spouse each day. Could just be going

to the gym or for a run or getting a pedicure, going shopping, getting together for dinner with friends, going to a football game with the guys. Charlie is so good about this with me and I have come a long way with him as well, thanks to him and his patience with me! I guess this helps us stay connected to each other because we realize we can be happily married and still be an individual and not lose sense of the person we were and the things we liked to do before marriage and children.

Addendum

*I*n a study of 700 adolescents, researchers found that "compared to families with two natural parents living in the home, adolescents from single-parent families have been found to engage in greater and earlier sexual activity."

Source: Carol W. Metzler, et al. "The Social Context for Risky Sexual Behavior Among Adolescents," *Journal of Behavioral Medicine* 17 (1994).

Fatherless children are at a dramatically greater risk of drug and alcohol abuse, mental illness, suicide, poor educational performance, teen pregnancy, and criminality.

Source: U.S. Department of Health and Human Services, National Center for Health Statistics, *Survey on Child Health*, Washington, DC, 1993.

Teenagers living in single-parent households are more likely to abuse alcohol and at an earlier age compared to children reared in two-parent households

Source: Terry E. Duncan, Susan C. Duncan and Hyman Hops, "The Effects of Family Cohesiveness and Peer Encouragement on the Development of Adolescent Alcohol Use: A Cohort-Sequential Approach to the Analysis of Longitudinal Data,"*Journal of Studies on Alcohol* 55 (1994).

"...the absence of the father in the home affects significantly the behavior of adolescents and results in the greater use of alcohol and marijuana."

Source: Deane Scott Berman, "Risk Factors Leading to Adolescent Substance Abuse," *Adolescence* 30 (1995)

A study of 156 victims of child sexual abuse found that the majority of the children came from disrupted or single-parent homes; only 31 percent of the children lived with both biological parents. Although stepfamilies make up only about 10 percent of all families, 27 percent of the abused children lived with either a stepfather or the mother's boyfriend.

Source: Beverly Gomes-Schwartz, Jonathan Horowitz, and Albert P. Cardarelli, "Child Sexual Abuse Victims and Their Treatment," U.S. Department of Justice, Office of Juvenile Justice and Delinquency Prevention.

Researchers in Michigan determined that "49 percent of all child abuse cases are committed by single mothers."

Source: Joan Ditson and Sharon Shay, "A Study of Child Abuse in Lansing, Michigan," *Child Abuse and Neglect,* 8 (1984).

In a study of 146 adolescent friends of 26 adolescent suicide victims, teens living in single-parent families are not only more likely to commit suicide but also more likely to suffer from psychological disorders, when compared to teens living in intact families.

Source: David A. Brent, et al. "Post-traumatic Stress Disorder in Peers of Adolescent Suicide Victims: Predisposing Factors and Phenomenology." *Journal of the American Academy of Child and Adolescent Psychiatry* 34, 1995.

Boys who grow up in father-absent homes are more likely that those in father-present homes to have trouble establishing appropriate sex roles and gender identity.

Source: P.L. Adams, J.R. Milner, and N.A. Schrepf, *Fatherless Children,* New York, Wiley Press, 1984.

In 1988, a study of preschool children admitted to New Orleans hospitals as psychiatric patients over a 34-month period found that nearly 80 percent came from fatherless homes.

Source: Jack Block, et al. "Parental Functioning and the Home Environment in Families of Divorce," *Journal of the*

American Academy of Child and Adolescent Psychiatry, 27 (1988)

Children with fathers at home tend to do better in school, are less prone to depression and are more successful in relationships. Children from one-parent families achieve less and get into trouble more than children from two parent families.

Source: *One Parent Families and Their Children: The School's Most Significant Minority,* conducted by The Consortium for the Study of School Needs of Children from One Parent Families, co sponsored by the National Association of Elementary School Principals and the Institute for Development of Educational Activities, a division of the Charles F. Kettering Foundation, Arlington, VA., 1980

Children whose parents separate are significantly more likely to engage in early sexual activity, abuse drugs, and experience conduct and mood disorders. This effect is especially strong for children whose parents separated when they were five years old or younger.

Source: David M. Fergusson, John Horwood and Michael T. Lynsky, "Parental Separation, Adolescent Psychopathology, and Problem Behaviors," *Journal of the American Academy of Child and Adolescent Psychiatry* 33 (1944).

Compared to peers living with both biological parents, sons and daughters of divorced or separated parents exhibited significantly more conduct problems. Daughters of divorced or separated mothers evidenced significantly higher rates of internalizing problems, such as anxiety or depression.

Source: Denise B. Kandel, Emily Rosenbaum and Kevin Chen, "Impact of Maternal Drug Use and Life Experiences on Preadolescent Children Born to Teenage Mothers," *Journal of Marriage and the Family*56 (1994).

"Father hunger" often afflicts boys age one and two whose fathers are suddenly and permanently absent. Sleep disturbances, such as trouble falling asleep, nightmares, and night terrors frequently begin within one to three months after the father leaves home.

Source: Alfred A. Messer, "Boys Father Hunger: The Missing Father Syndrome," *Medical Aspects of Human Sexuality,* January 1989.

Fatherless aggression "greater levels of aggression in boys from mother-only households than from boys in mother-father households."

Source: N. Vaden-Kierman, N. Ialongo, J. Pearson, and S. Kellam, "Household Family Structure and Children's Aggressive Behavior: A Longitudinal Study of Urban Elementary School Children," *Journal of Abnormal Child Psychology* 23, no. 5 (1995).

"Children from mother-only families have less of an ability to delay gratification and poorer impulse control (that is, control over anger and sexual gratification.) These children also have a weaker sense of conscience or sense of right and wrong."

Source: E.M. Hetherington and B. Martin, "Family Interaction" in H.C. Quay and J.S. Werry (eds.), *Psychopathological Disorders of Childhood.* (New York: John Wiley & Sons, 1979)

Eighty percent of adolescents in psychiatric hospitals come from broken homes. Source: J.B. Elshtain, "Family Matters...", Christian Century, July 1993.

"The economic consequences of a [father's] absence are often accompanied by psychological consequences, which include higher-than-average levels of youth suicide, low intellectual and education performance, and higher-than-average rates of mental illness, violence and drug use."

Source: William Galston, Elaine Kamarck. Progressive Policy Institute. 1993

Kids who exhibited violent behavior at school were 11 times as likely not to live with their fathers and six times as likely to have parents who were not married. Boys from families with absent fathers are at higher risk for violent behavior than boys from intact families.

Source: J.L. Sheline (et al.), "Risk Factors...", American Journal of Public Health, No. 84. 1994.

Children without fathers or with stepfathers were less likely to have friends who think it's important to behave properly in school. They also exhibit more problems with behavior and in achieving goals.

Source: Nicholas Zill, C. W. Nord, "Running in Place," Child Trends, Inc. 1994.

Kids who live with both biological parents at age 14 are significantly more likely to graduate from high school than those kids who live with a single parent, a parent and step-parent, or neither parent.

Source: G.D. Sandefur (et al.), "The Effects of Parental Marital Status...",*Social Forces*, September 1992.

Children in single-parent families tend to score lower on standardized tests and to receive lower grades in school. Children in single-parent families are nearly twice as likely to drop out of school as children from two-parent families.

Source: J.B. Stedman (et al.), "Dropping Out," Congressional Research Service Report No 88-417. 1988.

Kids living in single-parent homes or in step-families report lower educational expectations on the part of their parents, less parental monitoring of school work, and less overall social supervision than children from intact families.

Source: N.M. Astore and S. McLanahan, *American Sociological Review*, No. 56 (1991)

Children from low-income, two-parent families outperform students from high-income, single-parent homes. Almost twice as many high achievers come from two-parent homes as one-parent homes.

Source: "One-Parent Families and Their Children;" Charles F. Kettering Foundation (1990).

At least one-third of children experiencing a parental separation "demonstrated a significant decline in academic performance" persisting at least three years.

Source: L.M.C. Bisnairs (et al.), *American Journal of Orthopsychiatry*, no. 60 (1990)

According to a recent study of young, non-custodial fathers who are behind on child support payments, less than half of these men were living with their own father at age 14.

Families in which both the child's biological or adoptive parents are present in the household show significantly higher levels of parental involvement in the child's school activities than do mother-only families or step-families.

Source: Zill and Nord, "Running in Place." Child Trends. 1994

Forty-three percent of prison inmates grew up in a single-parent household — 39 percent with their mothers, 4 percent with their fathers — and an additional 14 percent lived in households without either biological parent. Another 14 percent had spent at last part of their childhood in a foster home, agency or other juvenile institution.

Source: US Bureau of Justice Statistics, Survey of State Prison Inmates. 1991

Seventy-two percent of adolescent murderers grew up without fathers. Sixty percent of America's rapists grew up the same way.

Source: D. Cornell (et al.), *Behavioral Sciences and the Law*, 5. 1987. And N. Davidson, "Life Without Father," *Policy Review*. 1990.

Only 13 percent of juvenile delinquents come from families in which the biological mother and father are married to each other. By contrast, 33 percent have parents who are either divorced or separated and 44 percent have parents who were never married.

Source: Wisconsin Dept. of Health and Social Services, April 1994.

Compared to boys from intact, two-parent families, teenage boys from disrupted families are not only more likely to be incarcerated for delinquent offenses, but also to manifest worse conduct while incarcerated.

Source: M Eileen Matlock et al., "Family Correlates of Social Skills..." *Adolescence* 29. 1994.

Seventy percent of juveniles in state reform institutions grew up in single- or no-parent situations.

Source: Alan Beck et al., *Survey of Youth in Custody, 1987*, US Bureau of Justice Statistics, 1988.

The relationship between family structure and crime is so strong that controlling for family configuration erases the relationship between race and crime and between low income and crime. This conclusion shows up time and again in the literature.

Source: E. Kamarck, William Galston, *Putting Children First*, Progressive Policy Inst. 1990

The likelihood that a young male will engage in criminal activity doubles if he is raised without a father and triples if he lives in a neighborhood with a high concentration of single-parent families.

Source: A. Anne Hill, June O'Neill, "Underclass Behaviors in the United States," CUNY, Baruch College. 1993

Fathers who cared for their children intellectual development and their adolescent's social development were more like to advance in their careers, compared to men who weren't involved in such activities.

Source: J. Snarey, *How Fathers Care for the Next Generation.* Harvard Univ. Press.

Sixty-three percent of 1500 CEOs and human resource directors said it was not reasonable for a father to take a leave after the birth of a child.

Source: J.H. Pleck, "Family Supportive Employer Policies," Center for research in Women. 1991.

The number of men who complain that work conflicts with their family responsibilities rose from 12 percent in 1977 to 72 percent in 1989. Meanwhile, 74 percent of men prefer a "daddy track" job to a "fast track" job.

Source: James Levine, The Fatherhood Project.

Twenty-six percent of absent fathers live in a different state than their children.

Source: US Bureau of the Census, *Statistical Brief* . 1991.

Among fathers who maintain contact with their children after a divorce, the pattern of the relationship between father-and-child changes. They begin to behave more like relatives than like parents. Instead of helping with homework, nonresident dads are more likely to take the kids shopping, to the movies, or out to dinner. Instead of providing steady advice and guidance, divorced fathers become "treat dads."

Source: F. Furstenberg, A. Cherlin, *Divided Families* . Harvard Univ. Press. 1991.

While 57 percent of unwed dads with kids no older than two visit their children more than once a week, by the time the kid's seven and a half, only 23 percent are in frequent contact with their children.

Source: R. Lerman and Theodora Ooms, *Young Unwed Fathers* . 1993.

Ten years after the breakup of a marriage, more than two-thirds of kids report not having seen their father for a year.

Source: National Commission on Children, *Speaking of Kids*. 1991.

More than half the kids who don't live with their father have never been in their father's house.

Source: F. Furstenberg, A. Cherlin, Divided Families. Harvard Univ. Press. 1991.

About 40 percent of the kids living in fatherless homes haven't seen their dads in a year or more. Of the rest, only one in five sleeps even one night a month at the father's home. And only one in six sees their father once or more per week.

Source: F. Furstenberg, A. Cherlin, Divided Families. Harvard Univ. Press. 1991.

According to a 1992 Gallup poll, more than 50 percent of all adults agreed that fathers today spend less time with their kids than their fathers did with them.

Source: Gallup national random sample conducted for the National Center for Fathering, April 1992.

Of kids living in single-mom households, 35 percent never see their fathers, and another 24 percent see their fathers less than once a month.

Source: J.A. Selzer, "Children's Contact with Absent Parents," Journal of Marriage and the Family, 50 (1988).

In a study of 304 young adults, those whose parents divorced after they left home had significantly less contact with their fathers than adult children who parents remained married. Weekly contact with their children dropped from 78 percent for still-married fathers to 44 percent for divorced fathers.

Source: William Aquilino, "Later Life Parental Divorce and Widowhood," Journal of Marriage and the Family 56. 1994.

The amount of time a father spends with his child -- one-on-one -- averages less than 10 minutes a day.

Source: J. P. Robinson, et al., "The Rhythm of Everyday Life." Westview Press. 1988

Overall, more than 75 percent of American children are at risk because of paternal deprivation. Even in two-parent homes, fewer than 25 percent of young boys and girls experience an average of at least one hour a day of relatively individualized contact with their fathers.

Source: Henry Biller, "The Father Factor..." a paper based on presentations during meetings with William Galston, Deputy Director, Domestic Policy, Clinton White House, December 1993 and April 1994.

Almost 20 percent of sixth- through twelfth-graders have not had a good conversation lasting for at least 10 minutes with at least one of their parents in more than a month.

Source: Peter Benson, "The Troubled Journey." Search Institute. 1993.

A 1990 L.A. Times poll found that 57 percent of all fathers and 55 percent of all mothers feel guilty about not spending enough time with their children.

Source: Lynn Smith and Bob Sipchen, "Two Career Family Dilemma," Los Angeles Times, Aug. 12, 1990.

In 1965, parents on average spent approximately 30 hours a week with their kids. By 1985, the amount of time had fallen to 17 hours.

Source: William Mattox, "The Parent Trap." Policy Review. Winter, 1991.

About the Author

*D*r. Wayne Parks grew up in Deer Park, Texas. Not long after graduating from Deer Park High School, he was accepted into Texas Chiropractic College in Pasadena, Texas and graduated with a Doctor of Chiropractic Degree in 2000. Upon completion of Texas Chiropractic College, he met and married his wife, Kristen in 2002. They have four daughters and reside in League City, Texas, where they home school their daughters. Wayne and Kristen have recently returned to school to complete a Master's Degree in Practical Theology at The King's Seminary, Los Angeles. Wayne is the director of Intersect 91 Ministry, which is a 501(c)(3) Non-Profit marriage ministry. This ministry focuses on refreshing and renewing strong and struggling marriages, as outlined in the Holy Bible. Wayne and Kristen have a passion to restore traditional marriage as this is the foundation of society.

CPSIA information can be obtained at www.ICGtesting.com
Printed in the USA
LVOW080830210213

320995LV00002B/5/P